THE
10 QUESTIONS
TO ASK FOR
SUCCESS

PHIL PARKER

HAY HOUSE

HAY HOUSE

Australia • Canada • Hong Kong • India
South Africa • United Kingdom • United States

Published and distributed in the United Kingdom by:
Hay House UK Ltd, 292B Kensal Rd, London W10 5BE.
Tel.: (44) 20 8962 1230; Fax: (44) 20 8962 1239.
www.hayhouse.co.uk

Published and distributed in the United States of America by:
Hay House, Inc., PO Box 5100, Carlsbad, CA 92018-5100.
Tel.: (1) 760 431 7695 or (800) 654 5126; Fax: (1) 760 431 6948 or (800) 650 5115.
www.hayhouse.com

Published and distributed in Australia by:
Hay House Australia Ltd, 18/36 Ralph St, Alexandria NSW 2015.
Tel.: (61) 2 9669 4299; Fax: (61) 2 9669 4144.
www.hayhouse.com.au

Published and distributed in the Republic of South Africa by:
Hay House SA (Pty), Ltd, PO Box 990, Witkoppen 2068.
Tel./Fax: (27) 11 467 8904.
www.hayhouse.co.za

Published and distributed in India by:
Hay House Publishers India, Muskaan Complex, Plot No.3, B-2,
Vasant Kunj, New Delhi – 110 070.
Tel.: (91) 11 4176 1620; Fax: (91) 11 4176 1630.
www.hayhouse.co.in

Distributed in Canada by:
Raincoast, 9050 Shaughnessy St, Vancouver, BC V6P 6E5.
Tel.: (1) 604 323 7100; Fax: (1) 604 323 2600

Previously published in the UK by Nipton Publishing

Text © Phil Parker, 2000, 2012

The moral rights of the author have been asserted.

The information given in this book should not be treated as a substitute for professional medical advice; always consult a medical practitioner. Any use of information in this book is at the reader's discretion and risk. Neither the author nor the publisher can be held responsible for any loss, claim or damage arising out of the use, or misuse, or the suggestions made or the failure to take medical advice.

A catalogue record for this book is available from the British Library.

ISBN: 978-1-84850-811-8

Printed and bound in Great Britain by TJ International, Padstow, Cornwall.

For the very lovely Natasha

Contents

CONTENTS

Acknowledgements

I'd like to thank so many inspirational people for their help and assistance while writing this book, especially my kids. I love you all.

Thanks go to the tireless Ros for editing and proofreading the first edition, to the magical Barbara for her peerless editing of this edition, and to all at Hay House for their brilliant support.

A heartfelt thank-you must also go to the pioneers of NLP and hypnotherapy who have inspired me so much, especially Milton Erickson, Richard Bandler and John Grinder, Connirae and Steve Andreas (especially for Q6), and Robert Dilts.

Finally, I'd like to thank all of my teachers throughout the years. Especially those who were appalling: you taught me as much, perhaps, by beautifully demonstrating how *not* to do it! You probably don't even know who you are.

THE 10 QUESTIONS
A Swiss Army Knife for Life

'A prudent question is one-half of wisdom.'
FRANCIS BACON

?????
?????

WHO IS THIS BOOK FOR?

Everyone.

Well, of course you'd probably *expect* me to say that, but these skills are so universally important that you can consider this a toolkit for success, in any area of your life. It's an essential instruction manual, a Swiss army knife for life.

This book is for you if you're interested in personal development and the pursuit of excellence, both for yourself and when working with others. It can be your own personal coach, or used in a professional capacity if you are a professional coach, therapist or business leader. You can use it to:

- design and achieve your dreams

- ensure that your relationships work well, flourish and are fulfilling

- manage your business more effectively

- satisfy your customers' and clients' needs

- be more successful

- break through areas of stuckness, blockage and conflict in your life

- stop recurrent arguments both within yourself and with others: your partner, your kids or anyone else

- sort out misunderstandings

- release yourself from self-doubt, negative thoughts and unwanted behaviours and habits

- communicate, be understood and understand others more effectively

- assist others on their paths away from conflict, wasted time and energy, and towards transformation and fulfilment.

HOW CAN A BOOK OF QUESTIONS BE THE MOST IMPORTANT BOOK YOU MIGHT EVER READ?

You might be thinking 'How can that be when it's just full of questions? Surely I want answers, not questions?'

While this is a reasonable request, it might surprise you to discover that the most important thing that I've learned from over two decades of working in this field is: *Providing solutions, advice, suggestions or answers doesn't really help much.*

Even more unhelpful, in particular, is unrequested advice, which is like pouring milk into someone's orange juice.

Some of you might have already discovered these truths and are looking for the tools and skills to ask the right questions. Wherever you are in this journey of discovery, whether you're new to this or have seen some of it before, you will gain new tools, new perspectives and, if you want it, a new life.

Let's start by reviewing why questions can be so much more valuable than answers.

WHY GIVING OUT ANSWERS DOESN'T HELP MUCH

First, the answers I might offer for your problems will be *my* solutions to them, and not yours. And although these solutions might have worked well for me, they might not be great for you. For instance:

Q: Should I marry that girl?

Advice: No, I don't find her attractive.

How useful is my advice here?

Secondly, if I simply supply you with answers then you won't go through the process of finding a solution for yourself. This 'finding a solution' process is essential in helping you to create solutions for other problems you might come across in the future. If you don't go through this 'finding a solution' process here, then when you get stuck at some future point, you're likely either to apply exactly the same solutions as I suggested before, which may be inappropriate for that scenario, or ask someone else for help. Asking someone else for help is a reasonable strategy, but what if there is no one around to ask, or if the only source of advice is not very helpful or just plain wrong?

You can see how this applies not just to working on your own issues but also to working with individuals, with teams, in business, a relationship or a management setting. Giving out answers makes the recipients more dependent on others, less able to make decisions and less in touch with what's right for them.

WHY ASKING QUESTIONS WORKS

When you begin by recognizing that you already have the answers to your problems, within you, then discovering those answers not only gives you the perfect solution but also trains you to overcome different kinds of problems in the future, and leaves you with a sense of feeling good about yourself for having worked it out by yourself.

This follows along the lines of the slightly overused, yet continually valid, management mantra 'Give a man a fish and you feed him for a day; teach him to fish and he feeds himself forever' (unless he's vegetarian, which means you haven't been asking the right question!)

Creating your own solutions allows you to be more independent and skilled at finding and making the right decisions for yourself. In the same way that the whole of English literature results from the skilful use of just 26 letters, a few well-chosen and thoughtfully applied questions can create limitless, tailor-made solutions to virtually any problem.

So the best way to sort out problems is not to be given the answers but to know what *the questions* are that will identify the most appropriate solutions.

I'VE GOT ENOUGH QUESTIONS ALREADY

This may well be true, but it will take more than asking just any old question to provide the answers you need. This book will lead you clearly through the process of learning to ask:

- **the key questions**
- **at the right time**
- **to get to the solutions.**

This is the real skill of this process.

The Questions in this book are some of the most powerful tools on the planet, collected from many of the major teachings in personal and spiritual development, business, hostage-negotiation, psychotherapy, NLP (Neuro-linguistic Programming), hypnotherapy, cognitive behavioural and precision communication. They are the cutting edge of personal mastery – prepare to amaze yourself as you unleash your power.

One last point: when you've asked the Questions and discovered the solution, then to get any benefit you must actually do something about it. Can you recognize what self-help books, diets and gym memberships all have in common? They're all brilliant starting points: a fantastic show of commitment and readiness to do something to make a change and put your life on to a different, more positive track, and yet... instead of making changes, many people just buy more self-help books until their shelves groan with brightly coloured 'Change now!!!!' paperbacks (and finally they often need to go on a de-cluttering residential weekend to sort that out). They often swap one diet for another, wondering why they're not moving forwards with their weight issue. And they curse the wasted expense of their annual membership to that fabulous gym – because, in spite of all their good intentions, they can barely remember what it looks like inside.

HOW TO USE THIS BOOK

This book has been divided up in to sections so that you can become familiar with the 10 Questions for success by using them through the natural process of the evolution of an idea, project or dream. The sections are:

- *Creation:* looking at your desires and dreams
- *Action:* putting dreams in to practice

- *Challenges:* concentrating on the obstacles that we might meet in any project or life generally

- *Smooth Running:* taking you through the daily management of any of your projects

- *Completion:* helping you to be able to say, 'Hey, I've done it!' and 'What exciting goals am I going to achieve next?'

I've found that the process works best if you read the book through from beginning to end to start with; from the Creation section right through to the Completion section. I've found that this is true even if you are in the middle of a project and hitting obstacles, as very often these problems can be ironed out by getting the groundwork of the Creation section really sorted, or using the tools described in the Action section.

For the impatient among us (and that includes me), you could begin with the list (p.vii) of all of the Questions and the signals that will alert you as to when to use them. However, please read the chapter related to the Question before using it; you'll see why later.

Finally, have some fun with the book – any project that's not got a good basis in fun and enjoyment is less likely to be achieved. I hope you find the 10 Questions as useful in your life as I have in mine.

PHIL

CREATION

QUESTION 1
What If?

'*It is never too late to be who you might have been.*'
ATTRIBUTED TO DINAH MULOCK CRAIK

SUCCESS THROUGH EFFECTIVE DREAMING

Do you practise the habits of highly productive, creative thinkers? They ask themselves this first Question of the ten – and we've discovered they do it in a very particular way.

When researchers[1] began to investigate the process of creativity and problem-solving, they identified some key habits that seemed to be shared by some very successful people.

Walt Disney, in spite of reputedly being appallingly bad at drawing, is an example of someone who used this process. His particular strategy for being creative involved recognizing and separating out the three different phases of creativity:

- dreaming up ideas
- considering the practicalities of putting the ideas into practice
- assessing the ideas for problems.

Probably most importantly, he would engage in just one of these phases at a time, separating them out so distinctly that he might spend an entire day at a time just dreaming. He called this 'imagineering'.

Just dreaming and nothing else.

If he found himself starting to pick holes in or be critical of his ideas (i.e. actions which belonged to the assessment phase and not the dreaming phase), then he'd stop and remind himself that today was a dreaming day. Experience had taught him that even if this particular idea never came to fruition, he knew that by just immersing himself fully in to it, his mind would flow on to somewhere else, in a new direction that he might never have visited if he had critically stomped on that delicate idea too soon.

If you are not happy with the word 'dream', just replace it with 'imagine', 'think', 'brainstorm', 'problem-solve', 'guess,' etc.

I'm sure you can understand the benefits of such a process, especially when you compare it to what most of us have been taught to do – you know the pattern:

- **We produce an idea.**

- **Almost instantly we swamp it with the weight of all the reasons why it can't work, all the problems inherent with it and the hard work it might entail.**

- **We resign ourselves to not bothering with the impossible, unlikely or difficult, discarding the idea.**

- We carry on as before, only a bit more hopeless.

This is a great recipe for creating stagnation, frustration and despondency, and tends to be contagious. If someone can't realize his own goals and dreams he may be less likely to support others who are reaching for the stars.

Using the previously mentioned 'Disney Strategy' of separating the elements of the thinking process so that they don't pollute each other is a great step forward. Having set the stage in this way for the first part of the creative process, you are ready to unleash the first of the 10 Questions. Q1 will free you from the crushing and stifling effect of negative inner voices like 'I can't do that' and will allow you to dream freely. Say hello to the 'If?' questions:

- *'What if'* and

- *'As if'* – normally used as *'Let's pretend, just for a moment, that...'*

The extraordinary power of these two comes from their ability to allow you to step beyond what you and others already think is true. By suspending limiting assumptions, your creative processes are suddenly freed up.

I'd like you to imagine the following scene for a moment. You and the most negatively-focused person you know are planning a fun night out:

You: Let's go to a nightclub.

Other: I don't like dance music.

You: *What if* we find a club that plays the kind of music you like?

Other: We won't be able to find one.

You: Yeah, but *what if* we could?

Other: That would be fine, but we won't.

You: OK, *let's pretend, just for a moment, that* it is possible to find a club that you do like. What else could we do before and after going to it?

Other: Well, if we're just pretending, then a nice meal first, a limo with champagne cocktails and a Jacuzzi to ferry us and the girls to…

Notice how the 'If' questions side-step the powerful blocking statements of that 'It can't happen' attitude and allow for new ideas to be created, where previously there were just relentless obstacles.

Here's another example:

Other: I'm sorry, but I just feel that I won't be able to say anything at today's meeting.

You: Why is that?

Other: I'm sure I'll get it wrong and look silly.

You: *Let's pretend, just for a moment, that* if you could speak at the meeting and everyone thought it was totally appropriate for you to speak, and no one thought you were silly at all, what would you say?

Other: Well, of course, if they really thought that then I'd tell them how I thought the project could be improved by…

So, the magic formula for using Q1 is:

- What's the difficulty? What do they want to do but can't or think is impossible? (e.g. *speak at a meeting*) = X

- Find out what's stopping them (e.g. *appearing silly*) = Y

- Let's pretend, just for a moment, that if you could (X) and be guaranteed that you wouldn't (Y), what would you do/what would happen?

From the above example:

'Let's pretend, just for a moment, that if you could *speak at a meeting* and be guaranteed that you wouldn't *appear silly*, then what would you do/ what would happen?'

And applying it to the earlier nightclub example:

'Let's pretend, just for a moment, that we could *find a nightclub* and be guaranteed that *it would play great music*, then what would you do/what would happen?'

When the difficulties (no nightclubs that they like, or appearing silly) are magically put on hold, notice how ideas appear like spring flowers after a hard winter? How creative would even someone like Leonardo da Vinci have been if every time he put a brush stroke on the canvas someone that he trusted told him all the reasons why he'd never succeed as a painter?

'WHAT IF?' ABUSES

It is possible to misuse this Question by using it as a question of regret, for example *'If only* I had/hadn't done that,' or *'What if* I'd not shouted at her?' This only gives you an opportunity to blame someone else or yourself, and we'll look at the problems of that kind of way of thinking and how to deal with it effectively with Q3. For now, all you need to know is that applying this Question to past events that can't be changed is only useful if:

- **It helps you to learn something about that situation**

- **That learning teaches you how to deal with it more usefully next time.**

For example, asking 'What if I hadn't lost my temper with her?' may lead you to see that 'not losing my temper' would have been a more useful way of dealing with that situation. You'd then need Q3 to help you find a way to achieve that. Again, notice that this way of dealing with events is very different from 'What if I hadn't lost my temper with her?' leading to 'She'd still be with me now and not with that idiot from sales', which just takes us down regret street yet again.

Exercise: Kick-start Your Dreams

There are some brilliant questions that I've collected over the years that use 'What if?' Some of the ones that follow have a sense of almost creating a little bubble of protection, which insulates you from the opinions and unsupportive harshness of the world. They give you a chance to try out new ways of thinking and new possibilities, like starting to learn to drive a car in an empty car park or field rather than having your first lesson on the motorway.

Others of the questions that follow help to remind you that we need to seize the moment and get on with our lives and dreams. Try them on yourself to kick-start your future:

- If I absolutely knew I couldn't fail, that I would genuinely and totally succeed at whatever I did tomorrow, what would I do?

- If I were free from all the constraints that keep me from dreaming and creating, what would I dream of?

- If I could make mistakes and not have to get it right all the time – and if that were OK to do – what would I allow myself to do?

- If I could dream up things, and knowing that just because I thought them up it didn't mean I had to

IF I ABSOLUTELY KNEW THAT I WOULD TOTALLY SUCCEED AT WHATEVER I DID TOMORROW, WHAT WOULD I DO?

actually do them (this is called 'the money back guarantee' question), what would I dream about?

- If what I am going to do today was what I would like to leave behind as the sum of my life's path, my epitaph, the summit of all my achievement... what would I do today? And what would I do tomorrow?

Write down your answers – you're going to need to have these ideas to hand for the Questions to come!

Dreaming is just the first phase of the creative process, but without it, projects and change will die on the vine. Remember, treat your dreams like little children: they need to be nurtured so that they can grow into all they can become.

SUMMARY

- Many of us have been conditioned to unintentionally stamp out dreams. Those familiar incantations such as, 'You can't do that' and 'That won't work' are good examples of this.
- Successful inventors and creators have a strategy for overcoming these objections.
- Q1 is the key part of that strategy.
- Q1 frees us from the unthinking oppression of ourselves or others.

Now that we have some dreams, we're going to go through the process of fine-tuning them, which is the first step towards ensuring they happen.

QUESTION 2
What Precisely Do I Want?

Alice: 'Which road do I take?'
Cat: 'Where do you want to go?'
Alice: 'I don't know.'
Cat: 'Then, it doesn't matter.'
ALICE IN WONDERLAND, LEWIS CARROLL

THE JOURNEY FORWARDS

Those final questions in the Question 1 chapter will have started to get your mind moving in new directions, but it might need a bit of help to make some sense of the answers. This is where Question 2 becomes really useful.

It seems at first a simple enough question: 'What do you want?' It's fairly obvious that you'll need to ask this of yourself before you start on any new project, but you might be amazed at how often people don't ask this, and how often they don't ensure their answers are well designed enough to be of any use. In fact, very often their answers make everything much more difficult.

Exercise: What Do You Want?

Start by asking yourself this question now, and make a note of your answers before reading on.

Now we're going to check your answer against some very common, troublesome types of answers. One of the most common of these is that so often people's initial response is a list of what they *don't* want. Many people are so used to thinking of the issues in their lives in terms of 'problems' that they will get very stuck trying to express their desires in positive terms, and will end up saying something like this:

Q: What do you want instead of being scared at meetings?

A: *Not to have fear, anxiety and dread.*

Q: And how will that feel?

A: *I won't have that horrible sick feeling in my stomach, my head won't spin like a crazy theme park ride and my face won't flush like a big red beetroot.*

You may already have recognized the problems that result from this kind of thinking, and as it's so fundamental to the rest of the book, and potentially your life, this next section covers the significance of speaking in negatives, such as 'I DON'T want to feel SCARED,' in some detail.

In this section we will consider what happens when you use negatives. You'll find that one of your secret weapons for success will be to become more aware of your language, noticing the way you talk to others and especially the way you talk to yourself (yes, everyone does talk to themselves and it's not a sign of madness!).

The problem with using negatives has everything to do with the logical way that the brain works when trying to process negative phrases like 'Not to have fear, anxiety and dread'.

As soon as you think about the words FEAR, ANXIETY and DREAD, your brain instantly works out what those things are by recalling everything it knows about FEAR, ANXIETY and DREAD. The effect of this stimulation of the areas of the brain that are in charge of FEAR, ANXIETY and DREAD is that within a few micro-seconds you start to get in touch with the exact feelings (in this case those of fear, anxiety and dread) that you were trying to avoid.

Exercise: Elvis

Test this out for yourself:

For the next few minutes, try not to think of Elvis juggling 12 purple monkeys!

Notice what happened when you tried to not think of it… you found that you just couldn't stop thinking about it.

The ability to answer the question, 'What do you want?' in negatives is such a common and habitual way of thinking for so many people that there is a good chance that:

1. You think this way quite often

2. It will take you a little bit of time to train yourself not to do it.

(The cleverest readers – that's you – will notice that I used exactly that kind of negative wording with the phrase 'train yourself not to DO IT'. This of course instructs us to 'DO IT' – negative thinking. You'll also recognize how common this kind of thinking is, and how we hardly notice it unless it is pointed out.)

The first step out of this hole is to develop an awareness of your language so you start to recognize when you are stating goals in negatives – the key words to watch for are 'not' or 'no'!

Watch out for the slightly trickier ones like words that start with un- or end with -free. Examples include unafraid, pain-free. Again, using these words works against us because they contain the words that trigger the very feelings we don't want.

Once we've spotted these negative words, the next step is to become much more flexible and creative with our brains and language. The purpose of this is that we start to use the words that will encourage the brain to get in touch with the feelings that we actually wish to achieve, rather than the things we are trying to avoid.

Exercise: Stating It in Positives

If your first answer forms itself as something like, 'Not fear and dread', think about what you might want instead, and make sure it's in positives. Try each of the examples that follow, then check your answers on p.198.

- Convert 'not fear and dread' in to something positive.

- Convert 'not to be made redundant' in to positives.

- Convert 'not sad' in to positives.

- Convert 'not helpless' in to positives.

- Convert 'not to feel bad about myself and beat myself up' in to positives.

- Convert 'not expecting everything to be difficult in to positives'.

In my work with both people with chronic illnesses, and the doctors and medical staff helping them, I've found that too much immersion into a world of symptoms and illness results in a lack of words for what they want. They are astonished to discover they have hundreds of words for the things they don't want: pain, burning, stabbing, gnawing, throbbing – and none, apart from 'free of PAIN!!!!', for what they actually *want*.

FAST FOOD TECHNICIAN

There is a second reason why negative answers can cause so much trouble. Imagine eavesdropping on this conversation at a well-known burger franchise:

Fast food technician (FFT): What do you want to eat, sir?

Customer: Oh, not a triple burger.

FFT: Excellent. So you don't a triple burger. What do you want?

Customer: And today I don't feel like a bacon-topped double cheeseburger, or onion rings.

FFT: That's fascinating, sir, but what do you want?

Customer: I don't think I'll have the extraordinarily reasonably priced kids' meal with free toy.

FFT: Good. But please tell me what you want?

Customer: I don't think I'll have a...

– and so on.

Not only does the customer not get what he wants, but you can also see how quickly he becomes quite irritating to be with and how anyone could be forgiven for becoming less patient with him or starting to avoid him?

And there is an even more important consequence of this way of thinking, which is best explained with a quick detour into brain science.

NEUROPLASTICITY

In its simplest terms, neuroplasticity describes the amazing ability of the brain to change, develop and grow as a result of how it's used. Unlike computers, whose circuit boards will fundamentally remain the same as the day they were built, brains can physically change their 'circuit boards' or pathways and the way various parts of them link up, and research suggests they can do it very rapidly, especially if the new pathways are repetitively used.

So, when we use the part of our brain that talks in negatives, we are making it more and more active – and through the power of neuroplasticity (put simply, 'if you use a part of the brain a lot it becomes better and faster at its job'), then thinking in negatives becomes much easier in future.

When you think about it, you can see that all change (which could be described as things we are unfamiliar with but would like to do more of) and stuckness (things we are too familiar with and wish to do less of), are governed by neuroplasticity. As a result, we'll be looking at how we can make this phenomenon work for us to make new habits and new ways of thinking natural and automatic.

THREE ELEMENTS OF Q2

The second of the 10 Questions is specifically designed to avoid the kind of thinking that is always associated with stuckness, difficulty and frustration,

BRAIN PATHWAYS ARE LIKE MUSCLES – THE MORE YOU USE THEM THE STRONGER THEY GET

and ensure we are really clear about what it is that we want. When written out in full you can see why, if you answer the Question as it's written here in its three parts, things will start to move forward.

I've broken the Question into its three core elements here:

1. **What do you want**

2. **precisely**

3. **– in positives?**

Answering each of these parts will make sure your answer makes change happen. But there are also two key rules to keep in mind that will ensure you avoid some of the other common causes of troublesome answers:

1. **all answers must be expressed as something about yourself, something that you can do something about**

2. **all answers must express a realistic expectation.**

Rule 1

For example if we compare these two answers to the question 'What do I want?' –

*   **my wife to be nicer to me**

*   **to work on developing my relationship so that it brings me greater joy and fulfilment**

– we can see that the first statement is obviously not something about you. Because of this it also suggests that your wife is the one who needs to change. Although that might be a reasonable and wonderful thing to wish for, that is something that only she, and not you, can make happen. As a result if you try to work towards the goal of getting your wife to change, it either won't work very well (people who don't really want to change, or are changing because someone else wants them to, rarely make good, successful or long-lasting change), or it will take a long time, as you can't really control her changing.

Rule 2

If we compare these two answers –

- **to be ten years younger**
- **to have the energy of someone ten years younger**

– clearly the first one isn't realistic, whereas the second one is at least possible.

If you've ensured your answers are –

- **what *you* want**
- **precise**
- **stated in positives**

– and –

- something about you that you can change

- realistic

– then you will have a very well-designed goal, one that will make you almost unstoppable.

Exercise: Q2

Using the guidelines above, work out how to create a brilliantly well-designed answer for this problem:

'I get bored and put off any project I take on.'

Turn to the answers on pp.198–200 to see an example of how you might go about answering this.

BRAIN-BOOSTING QUESTIONS

Now it's time to wake up and exercise (remember neuroplasticity?) those parts of your brain that you are going to need to complete your designated project or dream.

How Will You Know When You Have Achieved It?

What specific and measurable result will you get when you have achieved your desired goal?

Describing that in great detail will further boost those brain pathways that are in need of some exercise. Ask what you will be:

- **seeing** when you have achieved it
- **hearing** when you have achieved it
- **feeling** when you have achieved it.

For example, if your goal is to be a stone lighter, then the answer to the question 'What do I want?' might be:

'I notice my toned body shaped in the mirror, I see myself wearing those jeans I've not worn for two years; I'm saying to myself 'I've done so well,' I hear my friends and family complimenting me on what I've achieved, I feel my clothes fitting me and I feel confident.'

Creating this level of detail and clarity will speed up the development of those brain pathways, and the more of your brain that is working towards your goals, the quicker you will achieve them.

Exercise: Success

Write down your description of what it will be like to experience your success. Write it in the present tense – 'I look toned' rather than 'I WILL or HOPE TO look toned,' and remember to use lots of detail.

'CHUNKING IT DOWN'

One of the classic ways to cause trouble with this step of the process of change is to look at your goal and feel like running screaming from the room. When you consider the enormity of exactly what has to be done to achieve the task you've now set yourself, it can seem very daunting at first.

Stay calm if this happens. There is a very simple solution: break your goal down into achievable steps. This means you can avoid becoming overwhelmed and setting yourself up for failure by having unreasonable expectations for yourself.

Instead of 'I'll write that book,' for example, break it down into 'I'll just write the first chapter' (see also Q10).

Think of this as taking 'baby steps' and making the task easy; after all, why make it more difficult for yourself?

Is It Reasonable?

Another surefire way to get stuck at this point is to set yourself excessive or impossible goals, which you will be very unlikely to attain. You could squander all your efforts and energy on it, end up feeling useless and gain more evidence for the perspective that things never work out.

For example: 'I will earn a million dollars tomorrow.' If this kind of goal is part of your normal experience, then it's fine, but if it's a massively unlikely outcome then maybe make it more reasonable, while still being inspirational and motivating.

Equally, don't use this as an excuse to set your sights too low, such as: 'I'll never get a job that pays more than $4 an hour, so there's no point in even trying.'

Knowing what is reasonable is clearly a question for your own judgement and you must find the ideal position between the two extremes of over-reaching and selling yourself short. As Richard Bach said, 'Argue for your limitations and sure enough they're yours.'

ECOLOGY CHECKS

This section considers other important questions which, perhaps surprisingly, might seem to be a little bit negatively focused. Whenever embarking on a new project, there is a time for some reflection to make sure you are heading in the right direction and considering the consequences that your success will have on you and those around you; this will ensure you can get what you want while still keeping what you already value:

- What would you lose if you achieved your dreams? Or, what does your current behaviour give you?

- What do you get as a result of not fulfilling your dream right now?

These 'side benefits' (avoiding failure or looking stupid) are called *secondary gains* or *positive intentions*, and are often at the root of why an un-useful behaviour is perpetuated. There is an entire chapter (Q6) later in this book that shows you what to do to get around this. Resolving these self-sabotaging behaviours is often the key to a new future. For the moment, however, just note if you are feeling any sense of loss or upset at the thought of reaching your goal.

- **How could you stop yourself getting this? And, how could you sabotage this change in the future?**

This question may seem very negative, but it's actually very important for discovering any potential danger areas that may get in the way of what you want so that you can be ready to overcome them if they occur. As an example:

Q: What do you want?

A: *To eat more healthy food, and just eat at meal times.*

Q: And let's imagine you're on track doing just that, how could you sabotage that brilliant change?

A: *Oh, if I were stressed at work I'd definitely stop in at the shop on the way home and get a chocolate bar, or two, to cheer myself up.*

If you are already prepared and aware of future pitfalls, you can either avoid them or rehearse how to get out of that pit if you fall in it.

It's a bit like going to the Arctic and only packing a bikini. If you know about the cold you should pack the right clothes.

This will lead you to Q3: 'What can I do (to make a difference)?' But more about that in a bit.

DESIGNING YOUR FUTURE

Answering the questions in this chapter is very powerful for four reasons:

- It provides a framework for getting really clear about what you want in your life.

- It ensures you create new expectations for your future.

- Just by thinking through things in this way, you will be starting to make change happen.

- By changing your questions and answers, consistently, you are neurologically rewiring your brain – and when your brain's on side and working with you, change and success will be much easier to achieve.

With the degree of clarity that Q2 provides, you will, unlike Alice in the quotation at the start of this chapter, start your journey knowing precisely where you want to end up. Knowing where you want to get to also makes it easy to recognize when you've strayed off-course. This is vital, but unless you have the questions to help you refine your goal, you may be left with a developing sense of hopelessness and powerlessness, feeling you are off-track but having no idea how to get back on course.

With the degree of clarity that these questions produce, you can ensure that the journey you embark on is the one you want, that it's the most direct route to the end-point you've chosen, and that you won't overshoot or miss knowing that you've arrived when your reach your destination: *It ensures you create new expectations for your future.*

We're going to explore how this process works in a bit more detail. Central to understanding this is to recognize why we have memories – that is, what purpose memories serve.

MEMORIES

Have you ever stopped to wonder why we have memories? We have all experienced that they can produce a wide range of feelings – sometimes they cause us pain or upset, sometimes regret, and can equally remind us of happy times – but why do we have them?

One perspective, which I think makes a lot of sense, is that the main purpose of memories is that they are there to inform us about the world, to help us respond to situations to the best of our ability and not to repeat mistakes of the past. Looking at them this way, memories serve the following purposes:

When we see a potentially challenging situation coming up – for example attending an interview, our brain checks out what happened last time we were in this type of situation. This response prepares us to deal with a situation by re-using strategies that worked for us in the past. Unfortunately, it can also cause us to *have a future that simply repeats* the past. So, depending on whether you are drawing on positive or negative memories, you will end up with one of two possible 'predictions'.

Prediction 1

You start anticipating a forthcoming interview by dragging up lots of old memories of disastrous interviews. Drawing on the negative memories as a guide, you anticipate that the current interview is going to be difficult. Thinking negatively, through neuroplasticity, awakens those specific parts of our brain and encourages more of that way of thinking.

Prediction 2

If you use the process of going into the future and seeing, feeling and hearing what we would like to have happen, and what that would be like (see p.28), then, in exactly the same way, the brain stores these new experiences just like memories.

This means that the next time you anticipate or encounter a similar kind of situation (a forthcoming interview) your brain will look to the most recent memories of similar situations (which will be the new memories stored as a result of asking these questions) and predict a more inspiring future using these new and more empowering memories as its point of reference.

For example, if you start anticipating a forthcoming interview by recalling your new 'the way I'd like it to be' memories and fully imagining –

- how it feels to succeed in an interview
- what you hear
- what you can see as it happens

– then these positive memories will be used as your guide to what you expect to happen. As a result, you'll find yourself anticipating having more confidence, flexibility and success in your forthcoming interview. Just by thinking through the process in this way, you will be starting to make it happen.

The power of positive thinking has been researched for years. There are some amazingly thought-provoking pieces of research, such as the one concerning the women who took part in a drugs trial for chemotherapy. Most of those who were given the real drug lost their hair, as you'd expect. However, of those women who were given a sugar pill (placebo), but were told it was the real drug, 40 per cent also lost their hair.[1]

In another experiment, a group of volunteers was asked to guess the sequence of coloured cards in a shuffled pack. Those who predicted 'well' in the first run were separated from those who did 'poorly'. In following tests, those in the 'lucky' group performed better than those in the 'unlucky' group. Richard Taylor, the lead researcher, concluded cautiously that 'this data provides some empirical support for the popular notion of luck.' Could it be that some people were 'just lucky', while others were not? A second experiment was run in which participants from both 'lucky' and 'unlucky' groups drew cards without being able to see the results. The cards were instead read by an assistant who was instructed to tell the participants that they had done well, independent of what their actual scores were.

In this experiment, an interesting thing happened. When told by the (lying) assistant that they were doing rather well, the participants' actual scores began to improve. The more they drew and the more times the assistant told them that they had 'won', the better their real scores got.[2] So, it seems that maybe our 'luck' is actually dependent on how lucky we think we are.

SUMMARY
· · · · · · · · · · · · · · ·

- Fine-tune your dreams. Fine-tuning makes them much, much more likely to happen.

- Use the power of neuroplasticity to get your brain on your side.

Exercise: Q2 and Brain-boosting

Take your dreams and goals, which you produced from answering Q1 ('What if?'), and fine-tune them by using Q2. Then apply the brain-boosting questions to exercise that part of your brain that's going to work with you to attain these goals.

Notice how that changes how you feel about starting and attaining your goal now.

This then naturally leads us on to Q3.

▶ ▶ ▶ ▶ ▶ ▶ ▶

ACTION

QUESTION 3
What Can I Do?

*'Action may not always bring
happiness; but there is no happiness
without action.'*
BENJAMIN DISRAELI

So now we've got some dreams, and some clarity, it's time to make those dreams real and make them happen.

While just having the dream is sometimes enough to make it happen, usually some action is needed on your part. I know that this might sound pretty obvious, but not using our influence to make something happen is almost endemic, especially among those who complain that *things just aren't the way they should be*.

INFLUENCE

It's worth clarifying at this point what *I* mean by the word 'influence'. 'Influence' is occasionally confused with 'blame', and 'blame' is often also confused with 'responsibility', as in 'I should have influenced that,' meaning, 'It's my fault,' 'I'm to blame.'

In fact, 'influence' means something quite different. It means being able to use your abilities to take action to change something, and being able to make a difference to the way things turn out. It also means that if you've promised to do something and you haven't delivered on that promise, then it's up to you to influence things (do something) to make it right.

Imagine you're on a bus and the driver collapses because he's not eaten all day. He may be at fault and to blame, but he no can longer influence the situation any further; the only people left to influence it for the better, and take charge of the wheel, are all the other passengers on the bus who can drive.

Become the driver. What will happen as you take charge of being the influential person in the driver's seat of your life?

Exercise: Influence

Try this two-step process:

1. Take a moment to look at your dreams and goals, and write down a list of what you want in your life.

2. Now do those things.

Sound simple? Well, it is. There are only a few things that can go wrong:

- Not following steps 1 and 2!

- Things not working out quite as you'd hoped or planned. In this case, stop complaining (OK, you can complain a bit, it sometimes helps!), because complaining stops you being influential in what happens next. Ask yourself again, 'What do *I* need to make this work out the way I want it to?' You might need to look at Q9 'Promises' to help with this, and/or check for conflicts by using Q5, Q6 and Q7. It really is that simple.

So:

- **When you start using your influence for something happening but it doesn't work out as planned, ask yourself Q3**

- **Then take the necessary action that is obvious from answering the Question and**

- **Things *will* start to move onwards.**

Q3 is similar to finding the right tool for a job. Trying to bang in a nail with a screwdriver is going to be tough. Finding a hammer will make it really simple.

BLAME AND INFLUENCE

'Take your life in your own hands and what happens?
A terrible thing: no one is to blame.'
ERICA JONG

One way of ensuring that things don't work out as planned is by not using your influence to change things where you can, and also by spending as much time as possible finding out which people are to blame for the fact that things haven't worked out.

Useful targets for this are 'them', 'the powers that be', 'men', 'women', 'my partner', 'my parents' or 'my upbringing'.

Blaming is a really tempting idea when something goes wrong. I remember I once opened a cupboard in the kitchen and an open packet of pretzels fell out and spilled right into my cup of tea. I began to curse my partner and the kids for putting things in the cupboard in such a ridiculous way. Then I realized that I was the only one who had been at home since the pretzels had been bought earlier that day; that I must have been the one to put them in the cupboard in such a ridiculous way.

Notice how instantly I stepped into blame mode, finding a wrongdoer – someone else to get annoyed and find fault with.

Exercise: Blaming

Make a list of the people you've found yourself automatically blaming over the last few days:

1.

2.

3.

4.

5.

THE COST OF BLAME

Blaming is a great way to lay the responsibility for a problem at someone else's feet. However, blaming is a dangerous distraction and can cost us enormously in two ways:

- We create discord between ourselves and the people we've blamed. We annoy them and make them wary of us and less communicative. We alienate them, creating an 'us and them' situation when we really need co-operation, and we get into childish arguments with them and often end up saying hurtful and destructive things we don't really mean.

- By blaming we are saying that someone else was the cause of a problem; that their decisions and actions made it happen, that it is beyond our control to do anything about it and therefore that *they* are the ones who *must* change or make good.

Relating to it as someone else's problem that *they* need to deal with leaves us disempowered and without any real influence over resolving the issue. When there's nothing that we can do to make a difference, we are in 'victim' mode, where we may experience being resigned, apathetic, angry and frustrated – and ultimately powerless.

Whether or not the blame is justified is really not as relevant and useful as asking the question 'What can I do to sort this out?'

BLAMING IS A DANGEROUS DISTRACTION AND CAN COST US ENORMOUSLY

Asking what we can do to sort a situation out is a particularly useful approach for dealing with any relationship difficulties, and this includes any personal, business, community or even international relationships (conflicts between countries).

Most relationships fail because people spend too much time focusing on blame, fault-finding and asking the 'Why?' question (see Q4). If instead they spent their time and energy answering the question 'What would I need to do to make this relationship work?' or, perhaps even more usefully, 'What would *we* need to do to make this relationship work?', then the beginnings of a solution could be found.

Man: You've moved my car keys again.

Woman: You never bother to look properly

Man: Why can't you just leave my stuff where I put it? What is it, a genetic defect with you that you have to constantly rearrange my belongings?

Woman: Well, *you* can talk about leaving things where they belong. Do you really expect me to believe the TV remote control sprouts legs and emigrates to the sofa by itself every evening?

Man: There's just no talking to *women* like you; you want to have your cake and eat it – and, boy, does that cake show on your waistline!

Yes, bickering like this really can go downhill quickly, can't it? Now imagine the scenario unfolding with both parties using Q3 instead:

Man: You've moved my car keys again.

Woman: OK, we've had this conversation a few times so I'd like to sort this out and find a solution that works for us both. What can we do to ensure that your stuff stays where you put it and the house doesn't look a mess?

Man: Oh, OK...

A solution is now much more likely.

Exercise: Unblaming

Take the people on your blaming list (p.46) and ask yourself if you are ready to let go of this blame and find a solution or if you'd like to be annoyed about it for a while longer. When you choose to move on (which is generally recommended by most philosophical perspectives!), use Q3 to help you achieve a step forwards.

Warning!

Q3 can be horribly misused: you will really patronize and disastrously annoy people if instead of saying 'What can *I* do...?' you say, 'What can **you** do...?' This is effectively saying that the other person is at fault, that he or she needs to change. It creates blame – which, as we've already discussed, is rarely useful.

It's also important to note that this 'What can *you* do?' kind of question is, in fact, allowable if you are in a 'coaching' situation. That is, a situation where someone has very specifically and clearly asked for your coaching and suggestions for sorting out a particular issue.

SELF-BLAME

There are three fantastic ways of misusing this idea of 'being influential in what happens next'. They are:

1. Being over-responsible. This is when you take responsibility for things you cannot possibly be responsible for:

   - feeling bad because the weather wasn't perfect for your picnic

   - being upset that your best friends were arguing at lunch and feeling that you should have been able to make it OK for them

   - deciding to *make* someone love you.

You are not an all-powerful god-like being (sorry to break that to you). You can affect what you do in your life, but you have very little say over what others do (that's called dictatorship, by the way). This, equally, should not be taken as a limitation: you're amazing and can do amazing things with your life, but that doesn't mean you have to do amazing things *all* the time, or fix the world for everyone else.

2. Beating yourself up, giving yourself a hard time or berating yourself. Returning to one of the key points about blame: the question is not whether it's valid, or not, to give yourself a hard time, but whether blaming yourself is as useful in sorting out the problem as asking the question 'What can I do to sort this out?' Experience shows that it *never* will be! Remember, cursing your stupidity for using a screwdriver on a nail will not be as useful as going out and buying a hammer.

3. Collecting evidence that 'proves' you are a bad, wrong, useless or worthless person. Tempting as it sometimes is to focus selectively on times we weren't at our best, the same applies as above: many an unhappy, unproductive hour can be spent talking ourselves down – but will that be as useful in attaining our dreams as asking 'What can I do to sort this out?'? It *never* will be! (Q5, Q6, Q7 and Q8 may be very useful here.)

THE KEY TO SELF-COACHING: UNSTICKING STUCKNESS

I've coached some extraordinarily successful people in my career: explorers, rock stars and politicians. I've found that one of a coach's key roles is to see the potential for greatness within a person and remind him or her of it; even those who seem to have achieved amazing things in their lives can forget that about themselves – so don't be surprised if you do, too, sometimes. What follows are some really useful questions for helping you to get in touch with yourself at your best. Ask:

- **What would I need to remember about myself to help me achieve my goal?**

- **When was the last time I successfully dealt with a situation similar to this?**

The key word here is *similar*. Often people will limit themselves to recalling situations that are *very* similar. For example, imagine they have a problem trying to master a new skill, like a new accounting program on their computer.

They find they've no experience of working with accounting packages before, so decide they can't find a time when they successfully dealt with a situation similar to this one.

They get stuck here because they are focusing on remembering times that are very similar, if not identical, to the present one. They need, instead, to be focusing on times that were a *bit* similar. This should be possible even if they have never dealt with this particular type of computer program before, or may be new to computers and not even be sure what a computer program is.

To do this you will need to allow yourself some flexible creativity in your thinking.

For example, although this computer program may seem unfamiliar at first, most of us have probably successfully dealt with many new and unfamiliar things before in our lives, like gravity, learning to walk, kicking a football, sewing, driving a car, using a microwave oven and so on.

These questions help you to remind yourself of past successes, remembering how you've overcome difficulties and obstacles in the past and how you've found ways out of seemingly impossible situations. We've all done this; otherwise we would still be stuck at that railway station/bus stop waiting for that train/ bus that was late or cancelled.

Exercise: When Was Similar?

Take an issue where you feel stuck or blocked – one you are starting to feel hopeless about.

Ask one of these questions to find a way of thinking about it that helps you get unstuck:

- What would I need to remember about myself to help me achieve my goal?

- When was the last time I successfully dealt with a situation similar to this?

USING Q3 FOR DECISION-MAKING AND SALES

Question 3 – What can I do (to make a difference)? – can really come in handy when either you or someone else is having difficulty making a decision, whether buying something or choosing which restaurant to go to. Let's take a familiar sales situation:

Buyer: I don't know whether to buy this one from you, or that one from the other place I've been looking at.

You: Well, what do you need in order to decide?

Buyer: It's important for me to know I can bring it back if I don't like it.

You: We'd be happy to offer that to you. Is there anything else you'd need in order to decide?

Buyer: No, I'll take this one from you.

This kind of approach is invaluable for all sales situations. Most authorities on selling will tell you that the key to successful business is, perhaps surprisingly, *not* to sell as much of your product to everybody and anybody, whether they want or need it or not. Instead, top sales people will tell you that the key to success is in creating satisfied customers. They also suggest that a satisfied customer doesn't even necessarily have to buy your product to be considered a satisfied customer.

In fact, customers who've been helped by the sales team to realize that your product *wasn't* what they needed may be the best advertisement you will ever have. They'll tell their friends how straight you were with them, how you listened to what was important for them and how, if anyone needs the kind of product that you sell, that you're the people to buy it from.

On the other hand, customers who are sold something they don't want are likely to return it, complain endlessly, find problems with it or tell their friends how your company is one to be avoided at all costs. This holds true not just for the obvious areas of sales, retail outlets and marketing forces but also for any endeavour where you are 'selling' something.

It may be useful to expand your notion of selling from the arena of 'product or service' to include any situation where you are trying to get an idea across to someone else in a way that motivates them to take some action. This broader definition will include all sorts of situations that we don't normally see as 'selling' (encouraging healthier living in your family, going on a date, choosing which movie to go and see) and will help us to recognize:

- how so much of our time is involved in helping others to see things from a new and potentially more fulfilling perspective

- how vital it is to have 'satisfied customers' in these areas, too.

HELPING WITH DISTRESS

When you come across someone in physical or emotional need, a coaching approach (i.e. asking them 'What do you need to do to sort this out?') can sometimes seem uncaring or as if it fails to acknowledge their current distress. So, although it's probably ultimately what they need, it will not always be appropriate to use at this point in time; instead, simply and compassionately offering your assistance can make a difference – by asking, 'What can I do that would help?'

Notice we are not offering advice such as, 'You need to do this!' but instead we are asking a question that focuses the other person on both the solution and on finding the most appropriate route to achieving it. People are so often really pleased to be asked this when they are in need, because it:

- recognizes that they are in difficulty

- shows you care

- reminds them that there are some potential solutions

- encourages them to feel as though they are part of the process of change, that they are jointly creating a solution with you that will get them out of this situation.

REMINDING YOURSELF

Since this chapter is all about 'what are you going to do to make a difference?' you need to remember that you are a powerful person who can actually make a difference.

Therefore I am going to end this chapter by focusing on how amazing we all are. We can easily forget this, as our current society isn't that set up for acknowledgement, positive encouragement or optimistic predictions for the future. So if you want to feel good about yourself, you're probably going to have to do much of the work yourself!

Exercise: Being Great

The following questions will help you to remember how great you are, and identify where you forget that. Run through them now and use them whenever you feel self-doubt or feel you've come to a dead end:

- Where in your life do you need to remind yourself what you're capable of?

- What would you need to do to be fully prepared to deal with those times when you used to forget what you're really capable of?

- Where in your life do you need to remember what skills you have and what you've already accomplished?

- What would you need to do to be fully prepared to deal with those times when you used to forget what your skills are and what you've already accomplished?

- Where in your life do you need to recognize that you're drowning in blaming others or yourself, or complaining?

- What would you need to do to be fully prepared to deal with those times when you used to drown in blame or complaints?

- Where in your life do you need to take action?

- What would you need to do to be fully prepared to deal with those times when you used to avoid taking action?

- Where in your life do you need to recognize you are influential and powerful?

- What would you need to do to be fully prepared to deal with those times when you used to forget that you are in fact influential and powerful?

Make a list of times when you were:

- extraordinary

- successful

- confident

- calm

- creative

– and spend more time thinking of these times, as you now should know that this will strengthen your ability to be this way again in future.

OTHER WAYS OF ASKING Q3

These alternative versions of Q3 can help to get you thinking about your goals in a new way:

- What would *I* need to do for this to turn out as hoped?

- What can *I* do to influence how this turns out?

- What would *I* need to do that will make the difference?

– or if used in a coaching scenario:

- What would *you* need to do for this to turn out as you hoped?

- What can *you* do to influence how this turns out?

- What would *you* need to do that will make the difference?

SUMMARY

- If you have a well-formed idea of your dreams (Q1 and Q2), you will need to take action to make them happen and you will need to keep on taking action when things don't go according to plan.
- It is vital to recognize that you do make a difference, and that if you resourcefully approach difficulties you will overcome them.
- It's time to realize that blaming is the well-trodden path to inaction, powerlessness, being unfulfilled and being dissatisfied.
- Always ask, 'What can I do (to make a difference)?' If you do this, then things will work out for you – but you must be consistent when asking yourself this question.
- Don't allow yourself the luxury of blaming or dwelling on why things are wrong. Find out in the next chapter why you should rarely ask 'Why?' and to find out how to deal with it when you do.

QUESTION 4
Not Why, But How?

'We can't solve problems by using
the same kind of thinking we used
when we created them.'
ALBERT EINSTEIN

THE THREE-YEAR-OLD'S FAVOURITE QUESTION

Three-year-olds can have hours of fun just asking 'Why?':

Parent: It's time to put on your shoes.

Child: Why?

Parent: Because we're going out.

Child: Why?

Parent: To get some shopping.

Child: Why?

Parent: So we can eat.

Child: Why do we have to eat?

Parent: To stop us starving.

Child: Why?

Parent: Because we'd get ill and that wouldn't be nice.

Child: Why?

– and so on.

WHY ASK 'WHY?'

We've been so well trained to ask the 'Why?' question that we often ask it unthinkingly. But let's find out how useful it is. Here are some blocks to success and happiness that you've probably come across at some time or other. Imagine someone has just said one of the following statements to you. Ask 'Why?' for each of these and see what results you get:

- **I just don't love you anymore.**
- **There are no seats left on the last train to Paris.**
- **We haven't given you the job.**
- **I'm depressed.**

As you notice the kind of answers the 'Why?' question might produce, you can see that it is actually a very limited line of enquiry, as it ensures we focus more on the problem and less on the solution (remember Elvis and his purple monkeys from Q2?)

Sometimes 'Why?' will get us some vital information, like an answer to why we weren't given a particular job, but more often it will only get us 'stories' such as 'I don't love you anymore because…' or 'I'm depressed because…' or 'I don't know.' These stories rarely help us find solutions.

The 'Why?' question is an attempt to find out where it all went wrong, to identify the cause of a problem – but knowing the cause of a problem

THE 'WHY?' FOCUSES US ON THE PROBLEM, NOT THE SOLUTION

doesn't provide you automatically with a solution. Finding out why your car has stopped working doesn't make it start up again:

Car owner: Why is my car not working?

Expert: The starter motor has broken.

Car owner: Why?

Expert: The metal was weak in it.

Car owner: Why?

Expert: When the metal was forged it had a defect, and they didn't notice it at the factory.

Car owner: Why?

Expert: We checked the records and the quality-control inspector was having a bad day that day.

Car owner: Why?

Expert: His wife had been cheating on him.

Car owner: Why?

Expert: The other man had more money, more hair and paid her more attention than her husband.

Car owner: Why?

Expert: He did better at school, got a better job, his maternal grandfather's genes for hair in middle age were good and he'd taken the time to get to know her.

Car owner: Why?

We can see from this that, although it might be fascinating, the car still isn't fixed. 'Why?' also tends to focus on fault-finding and blame. These are great ways to create more conflict, divert your attention from what's really important and increase stuckness and inertia (see Q3 for more about blame and influence).

Which brings us to the real Q4, which we should use every time we feel a 'Why?' coming on: *'How can?'*

While 'Why?' thinks about the problem further and focuses on the past, such as 'Why are you depressed?', the 'How can?' question considers the future and offers solutions:

- **How can I get over this depression?**

- **How can I help you to get over this depression?**

Asking the right question is, of course, vital.

If we take the example of 'Why don't you love me?'

Pause for a moment to consider the *'How can?'* Is it:

'How can I make you love me?'

– or

'How can we sort this out?'

Perhaps it is:

'How can I make my next relationship work better?'

To make the right choice you will need to be familiar with the concepts of 'what you can influence' and 'precision and clarity' (and yes, you've guessed it, these are part and parcel of Questions 2, 3, 7 and 8).

Looking at the table below, compare the very different results that can be achieved by asking 'Why?' or 'How can?' for each statement:

Why don't you love me?	How can we move on from this?
There are no seats left on the last train to Paris.	How can I get to Paris tonight/ as soon as possible?
Why haven't you given me the job?	How can I get the job/ a job I want?
Why are you depressed?	How can I help you to get over your depression?

Notice that the 'How can?' answers enable you to make a difference instead of just being a useless observer.

Exercise: Q4

Your partner always leaves a mess in the house. You're annoyed and usually start an argument with him or her by saying 'Why do you always leave a mess?' Which of the following 'How can?' questions will make a difference?

- How can I really get the message across that having a clean house is so important to me?

- How can I help you to remember to tidy up?

- How can we avoid arguing about this again and stay calm about this issue while we sort it out?

- How can you be so selfish? (Obviously this one isn't going to work too well; it's actually 'Why are you so selfish?' in disguise! And, similar to so many 'Why?' questions, it is focused on the past and on blame, and not orientated to the future or solutions.

You find yourself saying, 'Why don't my dreams ever work out?' Which 'How can?' question will make a difference?

- How can I ensure my dreams do turn out as I planned?

- How can I deal with some of my dreams not working out as I had hoped?

- How can I continue to pursue my dreams even when some haven't worked out as I had hoped?

- How come I am so unlucky? (Again, this one is really a 'Why?' question: 'Why am I so unlucky?' and is unhelpful in its focus on the negative rather than on solutions.)

You are tempted to complain to an employee 'Why are you late again?' Which '*How can*?' question will make more of a difference? (note: the answer here will depend on the type of relationship you have with this employee):

- How can you make sure you're on time?

- How can I help you realize how important being on time is to your sales figures?

- You've been late a few times recently, how can I help you resolve this issue?

Notice the amazing life-enhancing power of the '*How can*?'

Take an issue that you're having trouble with and ask yourself, 'How can I use this method to resolve that stuck issue I currently have?'

SUMMARY

- 'Why?' questions often produce information about beliefs and opinions; as to the cause of something, they focus on the problem, the past, blame and fault-finding.
- 'How can?' questions are about direct solutions; they focus on the future and the possibilities for action.
- Use the 'Why?' question very sparingly, as it tends to produce large amounts of not-very-

useful information that will confuse the situation and deepen the problem.

- Use the 'How can?' question to create opportunity and find a way out of a stuck situation.

If you're after data rather than someone's opinion then the 'Why?' question will be useful; but before asking 'Why?' remember the broken-down car scenario and ask yourself, 'What kind of useful information is this going to give me?' If all you're going to get is a chance to assign blame or to hear a story referring to events that are now passed, then don't bother asking it! Remember: 'Why?' produces *data* but can get you into a useless *loop*; *'How can?'* will break the loop.

These first four Questions are all you need to clarify dreams and visions and to put them into action. So now we move into that even more interesting territory where we discover how to free ourselves from the terrible predicament of being completely stuck, bogged down and paralysed. Read on…

CHALLENGES

QUESTION 5
What Am I Making It Mean?

*'No one can make you feel inferior
without your consent.'*
ELEANOR ROOSEVELT

There is an enormous chasm between what *actually* happens, what we *think* has happened, and how we *interpret* those events. This interpretation is so often where we really get into trouble. This space between fact and interpretation is the land where we make things mean something. Unfortunately, the meanings we give to events are so often inappropriate and just plain wrong. Let's look at how skilfully we 'do' interpretation as a national past-time.

Exercise: Bermuda

When I was a child we lived in Bermuda. Every day we'd go to this beautiful, fantastic beach. The sea was the most amazing colour and to dip your toes in the water felt just wonderful.

Now, cover up the paragraph above for a moment and answer these questions:

- How did you imagine the beach felt beneath your feet?

- What colour was the beach?

- Was the tide in or out/was the water a long walk away or very near?

- What colour was the sea?

- What temperature was the water?

- Was the beach empty, crowded or somewhere in between?

Now look back at my description. As you'll see, I didn't mention any of these facts, but as you are a human being the chances are that you filled them in anyway.

I didn't say if the beach was rocky, sandy or shingle; you might assume that if it were sandy it would be between white and golden in colour (it's actually pink from the coral reefs).

I didn't specify the distance to the water, but you would have had some picture of that, too, and you probably had some image of its colour (turquoise). You would have probably filled in the missing details about the temperature of the water, too, and assumed it was warm or hot, because you probably think that Bermuda is in the Caribbean and hot all year round; in fact, it's not a Caribbean island and it can be quite chilly in the winter months.

We stray from the facts into fantasy so quickly – in this case, it's not too important, but in other scenarios it can have devastating consequences.

FACTS

Let's get clear what we mean by *facts*. We mean something that would be evident to anyone else observing the events; a list representing what had happened so that everyone involved would be happy to agree this was accurate.

The ideal state is one of an unbiased news reporter, whose job is to report events without making any judgements or comments, and just sticks to the hard data. For example:

- The Queen is climbing the stairs dressed in a red velvet coat.

This is factual and should be agreed by all observing the Queen's stair-climbing event. If we look at another version of what happened, though…

- The radiant Queen, who has a place in all our hearts, is gracefully climbing the stairs and is dressed in the finest red velvet I have ever seen, which sets off her exquisite complexion perfectly.

We recognize the basic facts have been added to quite a bit and now appear with the optional extra of 'added opinions'.

Exercise: Interpretation

We need to apply the surgical approach of the first version of 'the Queen on the stairs' to events that have annoyed us, stopped us, blocked and disappointed us, or where we feel we've been derailed from the pursuit of our dreams and goals. Use the table below to see how you could interpret an event in a number of ways, some of which are quite negative and others of which are more useful.

Cover up the 'What could it mean?' columns and think of suitable answers before comparing them to the suggested ones.

Statement	Fact	What could it mean? (negative about me)	What could it mean? (more useful)
Nobody talked to me in the office today.	Some of the people didn't talk to me as much as they normally do.	They don't like me.	They were busy.
		They think I'm boring.	They've had a fight with their wife/ husband/boss.
			They know me well enough to not have to speak to me all the time and know I won't take it personally.

These varying interpretations will make a real difference as to how you feel about yourself and the others involved.

Here are two ways to deal with this example of interpretation.

1. Find the Facts

It may be worth finding out which of these interpretations is the most factual. You could do this by carefully asking the others whether they were aware of not talking to you on that day, and if there was a reason for it that you should know about. This has to be handled very carefully and clearly, to avoid:

- **others feeling as though you are telling them they were wrong to do this to you (blame – see Q3)**

- **others clamming up and not telling the truth**

- **others feeling that you're being hyper-sensitive.**

Sometimes your more negative interpretations might be right (they usually aren't, though). If that is the case, you can ask a form of Q3: 'What do I need to do to make a difference (in this case, not be boring)?' The answer to this would need to be evaluated as to whether it is something you'd want to do for *yourself* rather than being something you'd do just because it would make *other people* happier (see Q3 'being over-responsible' and Q6 'conflicts'). You could also ask yourself, 'Is it important to me what they think?'

More usually you will discover that your negative interpretation of others' behaviour was completely mistaken.

2. Focus

You could stop your negative interpretations in their tracks and instead focus your interpretations in a specific direction by asking a version of Q3: 'What do I need to do to interpret this in a way that lets me continue with my dreams?'

In 1879, Thomas Edison (whose entire schooling experience lasted just three months) decided that it would be wonderful to create a cheap form of lighting which was available to all, through the new discovery, 'electricity'. He thought this was an important goal to pursue, as at that time the main methods of lighting were candles and oil lamps, which were major causes of death in the home. He was sure it was possible, but not quite sure of exactly how to make it happen.

He began his experiments in earnest, passing electricity through everything he thought likely to produce light as a response. When all of these failed to produce light, and having exhausted all of his initial ideas, he began working with materials that he had initially considered unlikely to work (ordinary household cotton was the first thing he finally got to glow). It took over 2,000 trials before he finally succeeded in inventing the lightbulb.

When asked later how he had managed to keep on going when everything he tried had failed, he replied, 'I have not failed. I've just found 10,000 ways that don't work.'

Imagine you're trying to get a financial backer for your project. You approach 20 financiers but they all say they're not interested. You might interpret this as meaning the project is unworkable and not able to be financed. But what if you were to ask, 'What would be the best way to interpret this to help me continue with my dreams?'

You might remind yourself that this is just 20 individuals' opinions and that there are 20,000 financiers interested in your field, therefore to assume you know that the entire industry's opinion based on just 20 individuals' response would be crazy.

This ability to find the positives and the opportunities in things that might not seem that positive is a skill that separates those who get on with their lives, achieve the things that are important to them and inspire others, from those who feel unfulfilled.

'Victory belongs to the most persevering.'
Napoleon Bonaparte

FEEDBACK AND PIGHEADEDNESS

Looking at this, I am sure you can recognize that there is also a balance to be struck between being

'I HAVE **NOT**
FAILED. I'VE JUST
FOUND 10,000
WAYS THAT
DON'T WORK'

insensitive to feedback and being over-sensitive to it. Your task is to weigh up the merits of the feedback you receive and decide if there is fine-tuning to do on your project or not. Q2 and Q3 will help with this.

Exercise: Look for Red

To make this exercise work you will need paper and a pen, and you will need to actually do the exercise as you read through it for the first time. Do not read through it first or it will not work as well.

First go to a room that you're not that familiar with (if you can't do that, you can still do the exercise, but it is best if you can go to a room you're unfamiliar with).

Take precisely 5 seconds to look around the room, noticing everything in it that is coloured red. You will need to remember these things, as you'll be asked some detailed questions about this in just a moment.

Now leave this room (if you can't leave the room, then just turn away from the direction you've been looking in). Write down all the things you can remember that were red in the room.

When you've finished, you can move on to the final part of the exercise – see p.199. When you've done that, read on...

Exercise: What Were You Making It Mean?

Remind yourself of a time when you were so sure you had interpreted something correctly, and your interpretation was negative, but later you found out that you were completely mistaken. For example, a friend seemed to be ignoring or being cold to you one day, you took it personally, but found out your friend was just preoccupied and hadn't even seen you.

Ask yourself what have you recently interpreted in a way that was not helpful for you? What else could that event have meant that would be more empowering for you?

Where in your life would you love to have more flexibility in your choice of interpretations?

SUMMARY

- We habitually interpret things and sometimes our interpretations are way off the mark and damaging to us because we actually believe they are real.
- We need to discover whether our assumptions are correct or not.
- As it's inevitable that we will interpret things in one way or another (remember that beach in

Bermuda?), then we might as well do it in a way that empowers us. Ask, 'How would I need to interpret this in order to move on?'

- We also need to consider the merits of any feedback we receive, and choose how we respond to it.

This is one way of dealing with us getting stopped or blown out the water by misunderstandings, misinterpretations or self-deprecating styles of thinking. In the next chapter we will explore another way to deal with stoppages and blockages, which is especially useful when we find ourselves at odds with someone else, or even ourselves, so read on for Q6, which is one of the most profound Questions you can ask, ever…

QUESTION 6
What Do You Want for Me?

'It is not the strongest of the species that survives, nor the most intelligent. It is the one that is most adaptable to change.' CHARLES DARWIN

CONFLICT RESOLUTION

This chapter is all about spotting and resolving conflict; it's quite an in-depth process, so take it in easy stages. The results you can get by using these questions will be quite magical.

Conflict, Winners and Losers

We've all had the experience of finding ourselves completely at odds with someone else about a particular issue. In this situation we usually roll out one of the following familiar strategies:

- **ride roughshod over the other person's opinions, or**

- **give up, saying it wasn't important.**

Both these strategies involve one party dominating and 'winning' and the other one submitting and 'losing'. The trouble is you then have a very unhappy loser who would like to come back for revenge or will try to reassert his or her 'righteous' position at some point in the future.

Bearing in mind that most of our disagreements are with people we continue to be in contact with after the conflict (consider divorce, office politics, arguments with neighbours, even trouble among nation states, etc.), it would be nice to find a mutually beneficial and healing way to resolve this kind of upset.

In many cases we don't necessarily even need someone else around to get into a conflict with, as we're quite good at doing it *with* ourselves. By this I mean those times when you find yourself saying, 'It seems as if part of me wants to do this – but another part of me drives me to do exactly the opposite.'

You've spotted an internal conflict when:

- you find yourself performing a particular behaviour;
- that you wish you weren't;
- but you seem powerless to stop it.

Common examples are doing things like:

- getting unreasonably angry
- telling yourself that you won't be able to succeed at something
- commenting negatively about yourself
- snacking when you're supposed to be on a weight-loss diet

- feeling guilty
- smoking

– and at the same time wishing that you weren't.

When you start to think about these times of internal and external conflict, consider:

- how fighting these battles steals our energy, vitality, peace of mind and happiness, and damages our relationships
- how much of our energy and focus is used up in battles
- what it would be like to have all that energy (currently caught up in these behaviours) available to us so that we can do the things we really want to with our lives.

Once upon a time there was a beautiful orange grove, which nestled on the slopes just below a remote mountain village. The villagers had harvested the oranges for as long as anyone could remember, and it would have continued so forever, until that disastrous day.

It was early morning, and appearing in a raised cloud of dust a troop of horsemen and wagons rode through the village, down to the grove, where they began to pick the villagers' oranges.

The villagers rushed to protect their crop; angry words were shouted from both sides; fighting broke out and a siege of the grove began. The villagers were sure of their ancient rights to the grove; the incomers were just as sure that the grove had been granted to their masters, in a faraway city, by the king himself.

While the arguments and the battles raged, the fruit fell to the ground and rotted.

A wise man came upon the village on his travels; the villagers begged him to use his powers of reasoning to make the incomers go away.

He gathered the leaders of the two groups together; he took time to sit and listen to each of them in turn; and when they had finished, he finally asked just one question: 'What do the oranges give you?'

'We need the juice, for drinking, cooking and selling at market; without the juice we will have nothing, we will die,' replied the desperate village leader.

'We', replied the incomer's leader with a warm smile of sudden relief, 'only need the skins, for they make the finest marmalade in the known world.'

Knowing they could now work together the two men embraced and the wise man smiled and wandered on.

The process outlined below is an elegant way to resolve these kinds of conflicts. It takes a unique and compassionate approach to understanding the real purpose and value of the behaviours or actions that are conflicting with each other.

This process avoids the danger of allowing one side to win and dominate the other, by instead working until a 'win–win' solution is reached. This resolves the conflict and creates an opportunity for collaboration between the old warring parties.

WHY DO TELEPHONES RING?

Keep in mind the similarity between telephones and the process we're about to go through. Their ringing is designed to be annoying, to get your attention, to inform you someone is trying to get hold of you. If they weren't noisy and irritating, they would fail at their job. But, as you've undoubtedly noticed, a phone stops ringing as soon as you pick up the receiver and begin to talk to the caller; it would be crazy if it didn't.

Why am I mentioning telephones? Well, your unconscious mind, which is often where these conflicts arise, is a very powerful thing. It will already have started to notice some similarities between what the telephone does to get noticed and how these parts operate. Simply keep the idea of the telephone loosely in your mind as you read on.

THE PROCESS

I've broken the process down into seven steps. At each step I'll explain what the purpose of that step is and how to do it, and for some steps I've included examples to make the points clear. Right at the end there is a summary of the seven steps. It may take a few read-throughs to get familiar with the process, as for most readers it will be a very new way of approaching things. However I think you'll find the time invested in learning these steps will be well worth the benefits.

Step 1. Recognize That There Is a Conflict

A conflict is always present when there is disagreement or disharmony between one or more parties/parts/elements.

Symptoms that will alert you to conflict:

- illness
- self-sabotage
- dissipated energy
- lack of a sense of humour
- blocks
- arguments
- truculence
- uncomfortable silences
- sulking
- a sense of being dominated
- lack of meaningful communication
- confusion
- circular arguments
- broken promises
- unfulfilled intentions, etc.

Step 2. Identify the Parties Involved

The 'sides' in a conflict can take many forms, from countries down through to companies, departments, members of staff, unions, management, individuals, modes of behaviours, desires, etc. Remember that there can also be internal conflicts between different parts of yourself. These can include a range of unhelpful behaviours such as negative self-talk, anger, illness, auto-immune disorders, etc. This is a whole field in itself, and you can learn more about the background to this from my other more health-focused books (see pp.190–92).

Often there are just two sides to a conflict, but sometimes there are more parties or elements involved. If that's the case, it's actually good news! The more conflicting parts there are, sapping energy from your life, the more energy and purpose you'll have once the conflict has been resolved.

Step 3. Heading towards the Solution

The solution to any conflict is to discover where the differing sides share a common aim. But before you rush in to find out what that is, you need to be quite considerate of how each feels towards the other – as the two sides may have been locked in conflict for a long time.

THE SOLUTION TO ANY CONFLICT IS TO ESTABLISH COMMON AIMS

Step 4. Resolution Starts

Resolution begins with a change of perspective that allows for understanding.

Internal Conflicts

These are conflicts with yourself. As mentioned earlier, they can often be identified by statements such as, 'Part of me wants to do this – but a bit of me wants to do that instead.'

There are some important points that you need to consider and recognize before going further:

- **There is a 'part' or 'bit' in charge of this behaviour, although it will probably be working unconsciously – i.e. without you consciously choosing to act in this way.**

- **Consider how you might have created this behaviour in response to a difficult situation, probably a long time ago when you were much younger.**

- **At that time, this was the best and probably the only sensible and appropriate response you could have made, based on your understanding of how the world worked, what was possible and impossible, your choices and role models.**

- **At that time this behaviour worked for you and it was successful on a number of different occasions at getting you out of difficult situations.**

- Ever since then it's just been doing its job, just as you asked it to do in the first place. In fact it's been astonishing in its perseverance, and determined in following your original instructions precisely for all these years, with very little thanks.

- So although it may not seem so at first, this part of you/response of yours has actually been working very hard for you and wants something very valuable for you.

Assure all parts that your intention is simply to communicate with them, to find out what they really want for you. You promise not to destroy them, excise them, break them or belittle them – you are on their side.

External Conflicts

There are some similar and important points that you need to consider and recognize before going further:

- Everyone involved in the conflict is trying to get something positive by doing what they are doing (this is called a *positive intent*).

- There *is* a way for both sides to get what they want and to avoid the wasted time and energy that a conflict would create for both parties.

- That they can both gain without losing.

- That a new solution will be better for everyone than the one produced by conflict.

Step 5. Recognition – Creating the Environment for Change

To create any lasting change, you need to set up an environment where the parties feel recognized and valued. It also needs to be one in which they feel they can trust that the process will be fair and unbiased, and one in which they'll be given an equal opportunity to discuss and be listened to. Without this trust, nothing will change or last.

The most effective way to create this is first to recognize that there is an important and valid reason or purpose behind each side's behaviour.

Internal Conflicts – Thanking

With internal conflicts you need to recognize where each part is located in or around your body. Do this by noticing where you feel the symptom that alerts you to conflict. For example, ask yourself 'Where is that anger, that sense of doom/hopelessness/fear, etc., located in my body?'

Let's walk through an example. You want to phone someone up and ask her for something (maybe something vital for your project or a date).But you don't phone her, even though you know that you ought to. We've all been in this situation at various points in our lives. So we have one part that wants to phone and one part that doesn't want to phone.

Begin by taking the time to turn the focus of your attention within yourself. Spend some time just authentically thanking the parts of you, one at a time, for just doing exactly what they have been doing, remembering everything mentioned in Step 4 and especially focusing on the fact that these parts/responses have only been doing exactly what *you* instructed them to do all that time ago.

You particularly need to help yourself to move on from thinking of parts of you as 'good' and others as 'bad'.

Take some time with this step; these parts have been working hard for you (for example, a part that is in charge of low self-esteem does a great and full-time job of pointing out examples of when you've not come up to scratch, and keeping your inner voice negative about yourself and anything you try to achieve). They've been doing exactly what you've asked them to do and most of the time all the thanks they get when they do exactly as you asked, is that you get cross with them. Now, most people do get annoyed with parts that make them feel bad about themselves, but look at it this way: you should, in fact, consider it quite rude to treat such diligent workers in such a thankless way.

When you think about it, you can see that even though that part's being rejected, hated and repulsed every time it turns up and does the job you asked it to do, it is so committed to achieving its goal (which was designed by you to get something really valuable in your life) that it hasn't given up. How many times would you have to be told, 'I hate you, why don't you just go away and die?' before you gave up on someone? How strong and committed would you have to be to keep on going in the face of that level of constant rejection?

That's what this part has done for you, all these years.

It may take a little time to do this, but it's important to spend as much time as needed to come to a place where you can genuinely appreciate that this bit of you doesn't *mean* you harm (although it may actually be *causing* you harm).

External Conflicts

With external conflicts, again you approach the issue in a similarly unbiased manner. First you need to gain agreement from all concerned that avoiding conflict would be useful and beneficial. Use the process outlined below to suggest how a mutually acceptable solution can be reached. (You might need Q1 and Q2 here to help the warring factions believe that resolution is possible: 'I know it's seems unlikely, but if we could resolve this, what would we need to do to make this process work?')

Let's walk through an example. John is angry with Sam for being late for a meeting, and this develops into a nasty atmosphere of spite and point-scoring, which prevents the meeting being very productive. Something has to be done to move things on, but it's not going to be initiated by either of them because they've got locked in a conflict with each other.

The first step is for you to ask *yourself* Q3: 'What would I need to do to create the environment that will help to sort this out?' This might include leaving the room for few minutes together with your warring colleagues in order to discuss the resolution.

Setting Out Your Stall

Taking a cue from sales techniques, smart shopkeepers know that the way to get people into their shop is to make it look enticing, appealing and exactly what their customers are looking for, whether this is exquisitely designed showcase windows or big, price-busting 'stack 'em high and sell 'em cheap'-stickered windows.

Successful salespeople, meanwhile, know that the way to get satisfied customers is to show them or give them what they want the first time. This includes addressing their concerns before they've even had a chance to feel disappointed that the product/service doesn't do what they hoped it might. Both salespeople and shopkeepers approach the customer from the perspective of 'How can I let them know why they should buy or want this?' Getting your 'display window' right will mean likely questions such as, 'Why should I bother with this?' won't even need to be asked, as you will have made the benefits very clear.

For example, in this instance (Sam and John) you might explain that you would like to help them sort this out so that everyone can focus on the meeting and can pool their extensive resources and perspectives. You could explain to John and Sam that:

- You are skilled at resolving exactly this kind of thing in a fair and reasonable manner.

- You will use a process that allows everyone to be heard so that the situation can be resolved to everyone's satisfaction.

- It's a short process and simply involves asking and answering questions that will achieve just that.

Step 6. Identifying the Common Aim

Remember, although this is the key question to ask, there are no short-cuts to getting here; my experience definitely tells me you need to go through the steps above, otherwise you won't have the full and useful attention of the parts or people answering these questions – and without that, asking them will probably be worthless.

There are a number of other ways to phrase these questions, which we'll take a look at in the examples below.

The main questions are:

- What are you intending to get, that's positive, by doing this? and

- When you have that, what will that give you that's even more important?

Internal Conflicts

Going back to our phone call scenario, ask the part of you that doesn't want to make the phone call (the Not Phoning Part, or NPP for short), 'What do you want for me that's positive through not making the phone call?' In this process your job is to keep asking the question until you get a reply that is:

- a positive (and not a negative, as mentioned in Q2 e.g. 'I don't want to be upset')

- likely to be similar to the reason the opposing side of you is doing what it's doing – in this case 'wanting to phone'. Of course we don't know exactly what that other part's purpose and goal are yet, but we can have a good guess that it will want to move the project forward to achieve fulfilment.

This is how it might go:

You: What are you intending to get, that's positive, by not phoning?

NPP: Avoiding being rejected by her saying no.

You: And what will avoiding rejection give you that's even more important to you?

NPP: I'll be safe from hurt.

You: And what will being safe from hurt give me that's even more important to me?

NPP: I'll feel good inside.

You: And what will feeling good inside give me that's even more important?

NPP: I'll feel like I can do anything.

Notice how the last two answers, 'I'll feel good inside' and 'I'll feel like I can do anything' were the only positive ones, and the last one sounds like it might be an excellent fit for what we suspect the 'I want to phone' part probably wants.

Now turn to the part that wants to phone (the Phoning Part, or PP for short).

You: What do you want for me that's positive through making the phone call?

PP: To get that financier to realize how great my idea is.

You: And what will that give me that's even more important?

PP: With the right backing I can really make this dream happen, I'll have a team, others who believe in my vision and support me.

You: And what will that give me that's even more important?

PP: Ultimately, a chance to do those things I've always wanted to do, use the profits of my venture for a home in the Caribbean, start a fund for the research into making solar energy affordable to all, etc.

Now that you have some possible shared goals, it's time to move on to Step 7, where you will explore recognizing the common aims.

If your issue is more about an external conflict (i.e. it involves other people), then read through the following section next.

External Conflicts

To recap our meeting scenario, Sam and John have become locked in a conflict as a result of Sam's continued lateness.

You: 'John, I know that your commitment to something valuable caused you to be annoyed with Sam's lateness, and I'd like to discover what that is so we can sort this out. Therefore, can you tell me what it is that you were intending to get, that's positive, by responding in that way to Sam's lateness?'

John: 'That he'd take more care about being on time and respecting others.'

You thank John for saying this. This is a very important part of the process: it serves to validate that this is the person's opinion and, even if you don't totally and personally agree with that opinion, that he or she is entitled to have it.

You: 'And I wonder if you could tell me, when "Sam is on time and respecting others" what will that achieve that's even more important?'

John: 'Productive meetings and a lighter atmosphere.'

You: 'Great. And I wonder if you could tell me, what will having "productive meetings, and a lighter atmosphere" produce that's even more important?'

John: 'More fun, the department would really be buzzing, better bonuses.'

You: 'Great.'

As with the internal conflict example, you simply keep asking the question until you get a reply that you recognize may fit with the other person's/side's likely positive intention. Again, in this case we don't know what it is yet, but we can have a good guess that Sam, like most people, would like better bonuses and more fun at work.

Turning to Sam, as the mediator you'd then say:

You: 'Sam, I know that there's a good reason for your being late for the meeting, otherwise you wouldn't have done it, and I'd like to discover what that is so we can sort this out. So, can you tell me, what it is you were intending to get, that's positive, by being late?'

Sam: 'I didn't mean to be late, but this really important call came through to do with the Denver deal and I had to take it.'

You thank him for saying this. Again, this is a very important part of the process: it serves to validate that this is the person's opinion and, even if you don't personally agree with that opinion, that he or she is entitled to have it. It's extremely important to be impartial in this process.

You: 'And I wonder if you could tell me what "making that important call" produced that's even more important?'

Sam: 'We can finish the Denver deal now.'

You: 'Great. And when you've "finished the Denver deal" what will that produce that's even more important?'

Sam: 'More time to focus on the next project, a sense of achievement, satisfaction and a happy team.'

You: 'Great! And when you have "more time to focus on the next project, a sense of achievement, satisfaction and a happy team" what will that produce that's even more important?'

Sam: 'Fantastic possibilities for new ideas, great team spirit, better bonuses and record-breaking figures.'

You keep asking the question until you get a reply that you recognize fits with John's positive intention behind being angry ('more fun, the department would really be buzzing and better bonuses').

Step 7. Reconciliation – Recognition of a Common Aim

In this step you now move on to the final phase, where you assist the differing parts to see that:

- It's now clear that they share the same goals.

- There is in fact no conflict – they've just been using different ways to get the same thing.

- It's natural and sensible for them to want to work together in a new and powerful way.

Ask the parties if they now recognize that they are working towards exactly the same goals.

Ask the parties if, seeing that they are actually pursuing very similar (and often identical) goals, they now recognize how they can be of assistance in helping each other to reach their common goal. Get them to discuss how this will work out and what it will be like to experience it (this is a bit of Q1 and Q2 again).

Internal Conflicts

The ultimate goals from our phone call example were:

PP: Ultimately, a chance to do those things I've always wanted to do, use the profits of my venture for a home in the Caribbean and start a fund for the research into making solar energy affordable to all, etc.

NPP: I'll feel like I can do anything.

You: Now that you recognize that you are both pursing the same goal, what will you be able to achieve as you work together, pooling your resources and skills, letting go of anything that now no longer serves your common purpose?

The final step of this transformational process allows for a reconciliation of the parts; this in turn brings a sense that these parts have actually always belonged together. Rediscovering this perspective allows the parts to join together and to access a whole new way of working together. This new way of working together will redirect their energies and attributes away from squabbling and conflict and into pursuing their dreams and hopes.

Over the last 25 years I've seen so much profound change occurring in people's lives and health just by taking some time to follow these seven simple steps.

External Conflicts

Sam and John's ultimate goals were:

Sam: 'Fantastic possibilities for new ideas, great team spirit, better bonuses, record-breaking figures.'

John: 'More fun, the department would really be buzzing, better bonuses.'

You: 'Now that you recognize that you are both pursuing very similar goals, what will you be able to achieve as you work together, pooling your resources and skills, letting go of anything that now longer serves your common purpose? How will a new understanding of a shared purpose help you to iron out the issues around being on time for meetings?'

Extra Conflicts

Occasionally there may be some sense of reluctance – or even a clear, obvious reluctance – between parts, people, departments, countries, etc. to recognize their shared purpose. If this happens then it simply means there are some additional elements of the conflict which have not yet been resolved. This is actually good news.

Imagine a team where two people are openly in conflict and another person is also not happy but is not bringing it up.

When the two-person conflict is resolved, things can move ahead, but any progress is likely to be blocked by the remaining undisclosed conflict. Once it, too, is addressed and resolved, suddenly instead of just having the combined resources and energy of two people working together, you'll have people working as a unit, pooling all of their efforts to achieve a shared goal, and then things will really start to take off.

As a result it's always good practice to ask, when you've reached Step 7, 'Is there any part of me/member of the team, etc. that has any problem with having this completely new and powerful set of relationships for building the future in a whole new way?'

All you need to do with extra conflicting parts, independent of whether they are parts, peoples, countries, etc., is to apply the same seven-step process wherever there is conflict. You'll find, with careful management, that these extra 'sides' to a conflict will respond to the seven-step process equally well. I have seen long-term infighting and bitter feuds resolved in minutes through the careful and sensitive use of this process.

Remember that, although it might seem that the most important part of the process is Step 6 or Step 7, the secret to its success lies more in the earlier steps, the changing of perspective and the recognition of the usefulness of each part/party; I'd always recommend spending more time on these steps than any of the other ones – I've found it's the quickest way to make lasting, easy change.

Alternative Questions

There are some other ways of expressing the 'What do you want for me, that's positive?' Question, which can be useful as it can be a bit of a mouthful. There are some complex linguistic reasons why it's designed this way, which are beyond the scope of this book, but all you need to know at this point is it is really effective at getting people thinking about things in a new way. As some people can find the Question a bit hard to understand, however, I've provided a number of ways of saying it that so that you have the chance to make it quite clear to anyone you are working with. Having these different options also means you don't have repeat the same question over and over again, which can sometimes make people think they have got the answer wrong, otherwise, they reason, 'why would you be asking the same question again?'

Internal Conflicts

- What does it achieve for you?

- What does it get for you?

- What does it allow for in your life?

- What does it produce for you?

- What does it want for you through doing *X* which is even more important for you?

- Imagine having that fully and completely in your life: what would that give you?

- Imagine a life where you are totally and fully experiencing that: what does that give you that's even more important for you?

- What does that give you that is so important for you?

External Conflicts

When dealing with external conflicts you can use the alternative questions above, changing the word 'it' for 'behaviours' and with the 'you' deleted or replaced with 'the team' or another appropriate phrase. For example:

- What does that behaviour achieve that's positive?
- What does that behaviour achieve that's positive for the team?

Warning

On the whole, this process is difficult to use in an external conflict where you are one of the fighting factions; your adversary might think the whole thing strange, or that it's some angle or trap you're setting. In these cases it's better to have an impartial mediator talk you both through the process.

Alternatively, you may possibly be able to sort your own issues out first (resolving your inner conflict, Q3–9) and come to your ex-adversary in a position to start afresh. You will have to be quite 'big' to do this and it may involve some apologies on your part, without necessarily being guaranteed any apologies in return!

Exercise: Conflicts

Make a list of any conflict within yourself or around you.

Resolving which ones would make the most difference?

Get to work using the checklist below. Some people find it easiest to follow a written checklist, while others use a friend to read it out to them or record the main questions and play them back to themselves as they use this process.

You can also ask any of the 10 Questions if you find yourself shying away from taking action at this point (I know your tricks)!

THE SEVEN STEPS – CHECKLIST

1. Recognize that there's a conflict.

2. Identify the parties involved.

3. Head towards the solution.

4. Change perspective.

5. Create the environment for change.

6. Identify the common aim.

7. Reconcile by recognizing the common aim.
   Check for any extra conflicting parts.

SUMMARY

- You can recognize inner conflict by its symptoms.
- Create a viable environment for change.
- Find the common aims of all the warring factions, through considering their positive intentions.
- Help them to recognize how they are after the same thing and that working with each other will always be better than fighting each other.
- The process is relatively simple but the delivery is all important and needs to be tailored sensitively to the individual needs of all concerned.
- Allow yourself some time to get familiar with the process, and discover how words are mightier than the sword.

> 'Man must evolve for all human conflict a method
> which rejects revenge, aggression and retaliation.
> The foundation of such a method is love.'
> MARTIN LUTHER KING, JR

We've seen how conflict can waste time and energy and can deflect us from our goals. The next two questions are vital for maintaining our focus during these distractions, and serve as a reminder of why we should take the time and trouble to sort it out.

QUESTION 7
What Is the Consequence of This for Me?

'There are risks and costs to a program of action, but they are far less than the long-range risks and costs of comfortable inaction.'
JOHN F KENNEDY

FOCUS AND RESULTS

'What is the consequence of this for me?' is a particularly useful Question for those times when you find yourself slipping into destructive behaviour patterns and negative thoughts. It's especially designed for those kinds of times when you feel you just want to give up or not bother to expend any more time and effort on something that's actually really important to you.

Warning Signs

Common signs that we are doing this are:

- sulking

- inertia

- arguing

- being childish

- raging

- complaining

- feeling resigned or hopeless

- saying 'It's not fair' or 'I can't' or 'I don't know.'

In this chapter we'll use the term 'behaviours' to refer either to doing those negative actions like sulking or to saying limiting statements to ourselves, like 'I can't'.

Exercise: Becoming Aware

Which of these kinds of behaviours do you notice in yourself too often?

Cost

These behaviours, although very tempting to engage in from time to time, always cost us immensely in terms of lost time, energy, satisfaction, friendships and the respect and trust of others.

Refocus

We have already described one way to deal with them (considering them as a conflict that needs to be resolved: Q6) but another approach, which is sometimes quicker, is simply to ask Q7:

'What is the consequence of doing this for me?' or 'What will continuing to engage in this destructive behaviour cost me?'

Allow yourself to list the *true* consequences of continuing along this path of destructive behaviour. Very often we don't allow ourselves to think about it clearly enough, in the same way that smokers mentally erase the warnings on cigarette packets and have amnesia about the fairly predictable long-term negative effects of their habit on their health.

Asking yourself Q7 ensures that you do take a good look at what you are doing and recognize the very real effect it is having on your life.

HOW LONG DO YOU WANT TO STAY STUCK?

Of course, the chances are that you will stop doing these self-sabotaging behaviours at some point in the near future; we've all exhibited these kinds of negative behaviours in the past and then stopped them later on, although sometimes it might have taken us a few minutes, hours or days to get around to stopping. So we know we have the ability to stop. The question is not 'Can I stop?' but 'How long am I going to indulge myself in the luxury of wasting time and energy and keeping my life from moving on?' After all, if you're going to stop quite soon, then why not stop now?

Nothing very productive is ever achieved in the time you squander engaging in these behaviours. At the very least you could usefully donate that squandered time to someone who could really make good use of it. For instance, you could spend it helping someone else who is more in need than you. You could even use it for your own learning: a new language, exercising or just enjoying yourself. When you add up all of the time you've used up engaging in these kinds of behaviours in the past, consider how many languages you could have mastered or how fit you could be by now if you'd just used that time more constructively.

Exercise: How Long?

A useful rule of thumb is never to indulge in the behaviour/s for more than 2 minutes. Anything more than that is just too long.

If you had only a few minutes or hours to live, or only a short time to spend with a friend before he moved to another country forever, how much of it would you *choose* to spend sulking?

Using Your 'NO'

Practise your ability to say 'No' or 'Stop' to yourself when you find that you're going down this route. Remind yourself of all those other times when you've said 'No' or 'Stop' just like this. Here are some examples to help you:

NEVER INDULGE IN **NEGATIVE** **BEHAVIOUR** FOR MORE THAN 2 MINUTES

- Imagine someone's just unexpectedly knocked into you, and it hurt. You instantly get annoyed and angry. Then you realize it was a small child and that she had done it completely by mistake and didn't mean any harm or offence. Then you see the look of fear on her face as she sees you raging at her. You recognize that your response is inappropriate. You *stop* being angry and maybe explain why you were cross.

- Perhaps you can remember a time when you were sulking about something but got to a point when you suddenly realized how pointless it was, how silly, and how you actually wanted to get on with something else, so you *stopped* sulking and moved on.

You will actually have thousands of examples of this, although the time lag between sulking and stopping may vary quite a lot!

The combination of focusing on the consequences of what you are doing and, if you don't like those consequences, saying 'Stop' or 'No' is a very simple but extremely powerful process.

I DON'T KNOW

Have you ever said this?

This one is a really sneaky phrase, is usually used inappropriately and is a disaster waiting to happen. It seems such a genuine sentiment: 'You know, I've really thought long and hard about the issue, and I honestly just don't know,' but it's really a snake in the grass.

Genuine Usage

'I don't know' should only be used when we don't have access to particular information, such as:

Q: 'What is the capital of Fiji?'

A: 'I don't know.'

In this case, 'I don't know' is a completely reasonable response, and if we wanted to find out we could then say, 'But I can look it up' (it's Suva, by the way).

Most of us, however, use 'I don't know' as a way of not answering questions that we do actually know the answers to; we just don't want to respond, for all sorts of possible reasons. Here are the top three most popular ones:

Q: 'What shall we do tonight?'

A: 'Oh, I don't know.'

1. *In case I get it wrong* – in this case it means, 'I know what I want to do, but I'm afraid that if I say it you might think it's not very cool, then I'll look stupid and get embarrassed.'
2. *I can't be bothered to answer, but I don't want to say that* – here it means, 'It's far too much effort to come up with an answer – you decide for me.'

3. *I think it's too hard to find the answer* – here it means, 'I can't face going through the stress involved in deciding – you do it for me.'

Above all, 'I don't know' is a fantastic way to avoid becoming influential and powerful in your life, and a great strategy for trying to make someone else come up with the answers for you.

Available in Many Flavours

'I don't know' can also come masked as one of these phrases: 'I'm not sure,' 'I'm not certain,' 'I'll get back to you,' or 'Give me some time to think about it.' The last two may not always be 'I don't knows.' Sometimes they are used when we genuinely need to take a moment to think things through or check some details before coming up with an answer. However, usually they are cunningly disguised 'I don't knows'. You'll be able to tell the difference easily, as if the person who says one of these really means it she will get back to you (see Q9 for real promises).

Cost

There are two main costs that result from using 'I don't knows':

First, the other person involved begins to get rather annoyed with your lack of contribution, enthusiasm, sense of purpose and the fact that he has to choose all the time. Additionally, there is an unpleasant little dance that goes on between you, the non-chooser, and the elected chooser. The steps are as follows:

- You probably did have a secret preference, although you never let him know it.

- You used your 'I don't know' to elect him to be the chooser.

- He got suckered into choosing for you.

- Unless he guessed your secret choice, then whatever he chose, however good it was, wasn't what you wanted.

- You tried unsuccessfully to hide your disappointment

- He knew you didn't have as good a time as you had hoped for.

This leaves everyone feeling a little bit jaded by the experience, as nobody will have had a great time.

Secondly, you find that you never really get what you want because you never tell anyone clearly what you want. You don't get to design your life, or express opinions as to where it's heading next, and instead someone else takes control for you. And no matter how well meaning and insightful others are, they could never, ever know as much about you and what *you* want and desire as you do.

Having others make choices for us leaves us feeling disempowered and like a bystander in our own lives.

I'd strongly recommend that you ban 'I don't know' from your repertoire right now, or if you do use it, follow it up with phrases such as:

- ...but I'll find out by (a time/date)
- ...give me a few minutes and I'll decide.

This is basically adding Q3 'What would I need to do to know/choose what I want, etc.?' to the 'I don't know' to move it from being a roadblock to being a path to the future. Asking Q7 'What are the consequences of not finding out?' will help to remind you of the cost of not getting on the case and finding an answer.

In the Office

In a business context, 'I don't know' is a killer. If you use it you will be written off as dead wood. Consider the following:

Q: 'Paul, what do you think we should do about the Boston contract?'

A: 'I just don't know.'

Q: 'Paul, can you have this project report finished by Friday?'

A: 'I don't know.'

Q: 'Paul, it's Friday, where's that project report?'

A: 'I don't know.'

– or

A: 'I really tried to get the computer to work but I just *don't know* how to do spreadsheets with graphical inserts.'

– or

A: 'I just *don't know* how it didn't get finished on time.'

Even in less obvious workplace contexts, it's still a killer:

Q: 'Where shall we go for the office party?'

A: 'I don't know.'

– or

Q: 'Will you come to the office party?'

A: 'I don't know.'

Using this phrase marks you out as being unclear and indecisive. People will be less likely to consult you about any decisions or to consider you as an important force in the organization. This is definitely not one of the seven habits of highly effective people (see Stephen Covey's book of the same name). Making decisions *is* one of the seven habits[1]. Compare that last 'I don't know' response to these ones:

Q: 'Will you come to the office party?'

A: 'I don't know.'

– or

A: 'No, I can't make that date.'

– or

A: 'Can I tell you by this Tuesday? I just need to check on a couple of things first.'

I've seen many people make the most enormous turnarounds in their lives by just zapping this destructive phrase. In fact, I'd like to start a campaign against this seemingly innocuous but poisonous phrase, and petition for its removal from the language – at least of grown-ups.

Working with Others

If a colleague has requested some coaching to help them out of this mind-set, using Q3 'What would you need to do to find out?' alongside Q7 and Q8 would be very helpful. Make sure that you're not the kind of colleague who needs coaching: avoid the 'I don't know' trap!

I CAN'T

This follows a similar theme as 'I don't know.' 'I can't' should ONLY be used when you are actually, physically *unable to* do something. For instance, are you able to shrink to the size of an ant? Can you speak Portuguese? (If you don't currently have this ability then it's acceptable to answer, 'No, I can't,' though obviously you could learn.)

If we use the example 'I can't focus on my work,' and we take the 'I can't' at face value, interpreting it as that person saying that she is actually incapable of focusing, then we have two obvious responses:

- **'Oh, well, if you're not able to focus on your work, then you're no use here and should leave.'**
- **'Don't be stupid, of course you can.'**

The first response usually produces nothing useful apart from a sense of annoyance, while the second one usually gets you into an argument.

Very often, 'I can't' actually means 'I won't,' 'I don't want to' or 'I am not sure how to'. And, in fact, as soon as we've seen it in its true colours, much of the work is already done.

Working on Your Own 'I Can'ts'

When you find yourself saying 'I can't' statements, ask:

- Is it an *'I am not physically able to'* statement? For this to be true, in the case mentioned above you would have to have lost the ability to focus, or maybe someone is holding your work and running around the office with it at great speed!

- If not, then I'm sorry to tell you that it's an *'I won't,' 'I do not want to'* or *'I am not sure how to'* statement. This means it's time to ask yourself Q7: 'What does saying "it's impossible for me to gain focus" cost me?' This will help ensure you recognize why you should to take action and not let yourself get away with staying in this stuck state.

However, recognition that you need to move on from this negative state is not enough in itself. You will need to have a plan and take some action. This is where you will need to ask Q3: 'What do I need in order to be able to focus on my work?'

Q3 is a great start for 'I can'ts', but now we have a total of seven brilliant Questions (Q1–Q7) to ask to help us unstick exactly this kind of blockage. At the end of the next chapter you'll have another Question and the chance to go through applying all eight to an 'I can't' statement, to see just how much more powerful your approach is now by having these Questions at your fingertips.

Exercise: 'No' and Change

Practise your 'NO.' It's a very powerful asset. Use it wisely to stop things that aren't useful, but not to block things that are life-enhancing.

If you find you spend too long in one of the stuck states mentioned at the start of this chapter, then be creative and work out some ways to make it easy to get out of your stuck state. For example, if you are too sulky (and anything more than 2 seconds a day is probably too much!), you could talk to your partner and ask her to throw custard pies at you whenever you do it. Well, it's just an idea! Make sure you stop saying, 'I don't' know' or 'I can't.' Although I, like many people, used to say them all the time, I don't ever say them anymore and it just makes life better and more fun. Try it out and see!

SUMMARY

- Use Q7 when you are stuck, wasting time or immersing yourself in self-destructive or pointless behaviours and at the same time not getting on the case and sorting it out.
- Q7 works by focusing you on the consequences of staying stuck and also on:
  - what is predictable, as a result of continuing to engage in that stuck behaviour pattern

- what the costs of doing so will be to you and others
- what you won't achieve
- what others won't achieve as a result of you staying stuck.

The next Question works on a similar issue but focuses instead on where you want to be heading.

QUESTION 8
What Am I Committed to?

'Whatever you can do, or dream you can, begin it. Boldness has genius, power and magic in it.'
GOETHE

Of all the important Questions in this book, 'What am I committed to?' is possibly the most powerful.

If used appropriately it can kick-start the process of surmounting any difficulties, resolving any conflicts and achieving the seemingly impossible.

In any of life's journeys there are times when we lose our way, forget what's important or get tangled up in things that distract and waylay us.

This Question serves to remind us where we are heading, why we are heading that way and why that is so important for us.

SO WHAT'S A 'COMMITMENT', THEN?

Committed and *commitment* are strange words when you look at some of their uses – for example, 'committed' can be used to refer to someone being put away in a psychiatric institution, and 'commitment' can be used to describe an important element of a long-term emotional relationship. The definition I use is:

Commitment: something that you dedicate yourself to, something that you will make happen, that you will ensure occurs, no matter what.

Now, this isn't a guarantee that what you are committed to will definitely happen (remember, we are not all-powerful gods, just fantastically talented humans), but by being committed to it in this way, we are so much more likely to get it to happen. We will certainly find ways to get around anything that seems to be preventing our plan from unfolding, rather than just giving up on it. Consider the following:

> 'Commitment is what turns a promise into reality. It is the words that speak boldly of your intentions. And the actions that speak louder than words. It is making the time when there is none. Coming through time after time after time, year after year after year. Commitment is the stuff character is made of; the power to change the face of things. It is the daily triumph of integrity over scepticism.'
>
> ATTRIBUTED TO ABRAHAM LINCOLN

WHAT ARE YOU COMMITTED TO?

Consider those things that you are committed to in your life. You can tell what they are (if you *really* are committed to them, rather than just saying that you are) because they'll be the things you spend most of your time doing, thinking about, planning and/or working towards. They are the things that actually happen in your life – and that's because you are committed to doing them, so you make them a priority, schedule them in, find the time to do them and get yourself in action.

Exercise: Q8

Make a list of what you are committed to in your life. I've given you ten spaces; you may need more or fewer.

1.

2.

3.

4.

5.

6.

7.

8.

9.

10.

Now check your list: is there anything on there that you haven't done, planned the next step for or worked towards in the last few days? If there is, then you're probably not really that committed to it.

You now have a choice:

- You can decide if you want to re-commit yourself to it and then ask yourself Q3: 'What would I need to do in order to make this happen?' or –

- You can decide that you don't really want the benefits of this in your life and that your priorities have changed. You then need to stop complaining about not having this/the things it might have led to in your life!

Please note, though, this is *not* an excuse to cop out and renege on your commitments just because things have become a bit challenging or the going has got tough; if you're really committed to the things on your list, you will stay focused on them even when things don't go the way you want them to.

Using Q7 and Q8 rigorously together on yourself will help you to examine your commitments and recognize:

- the positive benefits of going after them

- the cost of giving them up

- if you are cheating on yourself by pretending you didn't really want them all along. This one is a very popular excuse for giving up on what you've longed for. As you'll see later on, it's OK to let goals drop that you don't want to follow anymore, but it has to be because you don't want them rather than because they're hard to achieve – otherwise that is just an excuse.

'The minute you settle for less than you deserve,
you get even less than you settled for.'
MAUREEN DOWD

Exercise: Re-commit

Reconsidering your list of commitments, which ones stay and which ones go? Which ones need to be focused on more?

Q8 – A LIFE RAFT

Consider Q8 like a life raft that allows you to climb aboard for a secure refuge when life doesn't seem to be helping your dreams to flourish. It gives you a chance to regain your perspective and remember why you are putting in the work in the first place. The clearer your commitment, the easier it is to see the big picture, letting you separate the clear signals from the background noise and getting in touch with what's important.

Just Imagine...

Imagine having an argument with someone you love, or someone you'd like to have a good working relationship with.

Imagine what would happen if you just stopped and asked yourself 'Is what I'm doing right now forwarding what I say I'm committed to?' How much easier would that make it for you to:

- **recognize the relative insignificance of arguing this point against the larger prize of developing your relationship?**

- **stop that argument more quickly?**

It doesn't mean that there won't be disagreements – there will be – but sorting them out by using Q8 will be much more productive than arguing them into a win–lose solution.

WORKING WITH OTHERS

In the coaching environment, Q8 is used in a very similar way to Q7. It is a good idea to check someone's commitment when you recognize he is stuck or not working on the goals that he has declared are important to him. Using Q8 will result in either:

- **a fresh re-energization of commitment and an impetus to action**

IS
WHAT
I'M **DOING**
RIGHT NOW
FORWARDING
WHAT I SAY I'M
COMMITTED TO?

- a realization that a particular goal is no longer that important and, if that is really the case, an understanding that it's OK to let it go.

LETTING GO – GOAL OR MILLSTONE?

Sometimes people will discover through this Question that the goals they had been working towards are no longer what they really want in their lives, but they've felt obliged to continue on regardless of their changed outlook. Recognizing that times have moved on, that goals and horizons do change and that it's OK to let those old dreams go can be a very freeing experience.

I have a good friend who always dreamed of emigrating to another country to start a new life with his young family. Finally their plans came to fruition: they sold their house, car and business and, with a big send-off, flew off to their new life. Within a year they'd come back. I was so proud of them; it takes a lot of courage to make such a move, and even more to realize that it wasn't right for you in the end.

Goals should inspire, not stifle.

Exercise: What Fires You Up?

Spend some time thinking about what you're really committed to. What fires you up? What would get you up in the morning with a smile on your face?

Ask yourself, 'What would I love to do so much with my life that, if it was available to buy, I'd pay money to do it?'

Spend some time really getting in touch with these powerful feelings. Every day.

SUMMARY

- Q8 is simple but extremely powerful. It acts like rocket fuel to refocus and re-inspire you.
- It can help you to realize that you may no longer be committed to what you used to be committed to. This allows you to refocus your energies on those things that are really important to you.
- Don't use it to cop out or give up by saying, 'It was never really that important to me anyway.'

Q1–Q8 REVISITED

Now that you've taken stock, refocused and are ready to do whatever it takes to achieve your goals, let's look at how we can ensure that we (or others involved) do something about it... but before that, we're going to remind ourselves of what we've covered so far...

Applying the First Eight Questions

This section is designed to help you become more familiar with the previous eight Questions by seeing how each could be applied to a single issue.

I'd recommend that, as you look through each of the Questions below, you consider how you would use that Question to help move the problem along. Then compare your ideas to what I've written. Hopefully they'll be quite similar, but if not, work out whether one approach is more useful than the other, or if they both work.

Imagine someone asks you for help; they tell you they're having trouble getting on with their work.

Client: 'I can't focus on my work.'

Q1: What If?

Now, with the first eight of the 10 Questions at your disposal, you have a number of obvious options.

Q1 can be called on to assist the client in seeing new possibilities:

You: 'OK, let's pretend for a moment that you have found a way to focus on your work. What would happen then? What would that be like?'

Client: 'That would be great, it would just be a breeze and I'd create something really inspirational with this project.'

Notice how the client's block has already started to disappear.

Q2: What Precisely Do I Want?

You: 'What would you love to feel about this project rather than "unfocused"?'

Client: 'I'd like to see it clearly and know which thing to do first.'

Notice how the client is already producing a game plan to move things forward.

Q3: What Can I Do?

As discussed earlier, you can recognize this 'I can't' as actually meaning, 'I won't', or 'I don't want to' or 'I am not sure how to'. This makes it an ideal opportunity to use Q3:

You: 'What can you do to be able to focus on your work?'

Client: 'I could stay calm, see everything much more clearly and then I'd know which thing to do first, and then I'd do the thing that tops the list.'

The first beginnings of a commitment to action are showing here. If the client does these things, he is going to start resolving the work problems quite rapidly.

Q4: Not Why, But How?

This will be essential if the client is stuck with the 'Why can't I focus on my work?' question.

Client: 'Why can't I focus on my work?'

You: 'Maybe we should begin with a different question instead. How can you get focused on your work?'

Client: 'OK. How? Well... I'll need to prioritize the jobs I need to do, take some more breaks, etc.'

Asking the right question steers the client safely away from the endless loop of 'Why?' and helps him begin to consider solutions to the problem.

Q5: What Am I Making It Mean?

If you have also discovered the client's reason for 'why I can't focus', then Q5 (pp.77–89) will come in very useful.

For example, if the client feels 'It's because the work is just too hard,' then using Q5 along with what you've learned about whether the client is seeing it in an accurate and useful way will help him to move forwards.

You: 'What is it about the work that makes it *seem* difficult for you to focus on it?' (Or, put more succinctly, 'Why is that?' This is one of the few valuable uses of 'Why?'!)

Client: 'Because it looks really hard.'

You: 'How else could you see it that would make it easy to do?'

Client: 'Well, I guess if I saw it as just a series of things to do, things that I've actually already done before as part of different projects, it would be less daunting.'

Q6: What Do You Want for Me?

This Question looks at the problem from the perspective that there is a conflict between how one part of the client feels about doing it *(I can't focus)* and how he wants to feel about it *(do it easily)*. Run through the 'resolving conflict' process (just as in the example of not wanting to make phone calls, p.108) to identify what is driving the person to say, 'I can't.' This will allow him to discover how that powerful force, which is currently being used to stop him, can be harnessed to propel him forward.

Q7: What Is the Consequence of This for Me?

Just by asking the client to look at the consequences of the statement 'I can't' will help him to change this stuck state of affairs. Carefully and sensitively it asks the person to recognize that he needs to do something about this other than just complain:

You: 'I know it seems that way but, when you really look at it, what does saying "It's impossible to gain focus" cost you?'

Client: 'It means it will be hard work, a struggle, and I'll be noticed in the office as someone who is not up to speed.'

Q8: What Am I Committed to?

You: 'I know how it is to feel like you can't focus on your work, but if you want to get through this and move forwards, you need stay focused on the bigger picture. The easiest way to do this is to ask yourself, "What am I committed to?"'

Client: 'To being the best in my field.'

You: 'And now you've said this and reminded yourself of it, how do you feel about getting back to being focused, and what are you going to do to make a difference?'

Client: 'Great – ready to go, to break it down and beat this.'

Here we can see the client recognizing the detrimental effect of relating to work as 'difficult'. We've then included Q3, which helps the client move on to taking some action to create change.

Using These Questions with Yourself and Others

In a coaching scenario (i.e. working with others), we would probably ask the Questions in a different order (for example we might ask Q3 before Q7). This is because Q7 is quite a tough Question. It really takes what you are doing and makes you hold it right up against your face and asks you to look at it, and that's not always very comfortable.

In a coaching situation this may just irritate the client, so we'd do it a bit more politely. When dealing with your own stuff, however, there can be no pretence that you haven't realized what you have been doing, so you can be a bit more up-front with yourself. However, do remember to be kind to yourself as well, and proceed compassionately (see the section on self-blame in Q3, pp.51–52).

You might wonder why you need all eight Questions if each one individually can be applied to the same issues. There are two reasons for this:

First, some Questions are more appropriate to certain issues than others. If someone says 'I have a part of me that is in conflict with another part of me,' then Q7 is your automatic Question of choice.

Secondly, the more Questions you have, the more approaches you will be able to produce in response to any given stuckness; that is the true secret of resolving stuckness. If you can be more flexible and creative at finding solutions than the person stuck is at finding obstacles and blocks, then you will always be a catalyst for effective change.

SMOOTH
RUNNING

QUESTION 9
What Exactly, by When, by Whom?

'I will always love you. The cheque's in the post. Of course I'll respect you in the morning.'
GREAT LIES OF OUR TIME,
AN IMAGINARY BOOK BY PHIL PARKER

PROMISES AND AGREEMENTS

Most of us are quite poor at making effective promises and agreements. We think a promise or an agreement is something like:

- I'll phone you.

- I'll definitely have it finished very soon.

I would argue, though, that these kinds of statements can't really be classed as promises or agreements because they are missing some basic essential components. Without these components an agreement has very little value.

I'd define a promise or an agreement as: *A contract that is clear to all involved parties and has a specific, measurable result that can be verified at a certain date.*

The shorter version is: *A clear agreement, with measurable results and a date.* The shortest version is Q9: *What exactly, by when, by whom?*

MISSING INGREDIENTS

Election time and advertising present fantastic opportunities to see non-promises at their best. Here's a good example of this kind of genius at work: 'We agree to specifically improve the services in real terms.'

This leaves out exactly which services are to be affected, exactly how they will be improved, by how much and by when.

Another example might be: 'We guarantee 100 per cent that this is the best money can buy.'

Reasonably you could ask yourself, 'The best in exactly what way?' You might also notice that the claim is absolute and unending in its scope, suggesting that it will always be true in every situation, and you will quickly start to realize that this is very unlikely to be true.

Exercise: Missing Bits

Look again at the first examples at the start of this chapter, and notice what is missing to make these good-quality promises:

- I'll phone you.

- I'll definitely have it finished very soon.

Answers

We can notice they both miss out the 'By when' part of the agreement. 'Soon' is so undefined that it will mean very different things even to any two people. These types of loose half-promises can lead to:

- **The person who thought she'd been given a clear promise being left with a sense of being let down, thinking that the promiser is unreliable, and**

- **The person who made the half-promise feeling that she's been misunderstood and that the other person is being unreasonable and expecting things that were never agreed to.**

And, unfortunately, upset and arguments will surely follow.

THE PROMISE OF THINGS TO COME

Let's look at a common example. Imagine it's a Monday and your boss asks:

Boss: 'Have you finished the project? I need it urgently.'

You: 'I'll definitely have it finished very soon, it just needs a bit of fine-tuning: it'll be done in less than a few more hours.'

Your boss goes away happy that, as far as he's concerned, he'll have it on his desk in time for Friday's meeting.

But can you notice what has gone wrong here?

Later That Week...

A few days later it's Friday and the following happens:

Boss: 'Where's that project you promised? I'm counting on it for this morning's presentation.'

You: 'It's nearly finished.'

Boss: 'But you said you'd finish it by the end of the week.'

You: 'No, I didn't. I said I'd finish it soon.'

Amazingly this kind of miscommunication happens a lot in business. It may seem like common sense to make proper promises, but it seems that 300 years after Voltaire first noted that 'Common sense is not so common,' he's still spot on.

If we look at this communication through the Q9 concept of real promises, we can straighten it out. We must have all the elements:

- **Step 1: asking for specific things to be done**

- **Step 2: setting a specific end-point by which time that thing will be delivered**

- Step 3: ensuring that all the people involved understand what they have promised to do (the check stage).

Exercise: Smart Boss

Using Q9, what do you think the boss should have said instead?

TAKE TWO

Our boss's goal is to have that project ready for Friday morning's presentation. Therefore, the new communication should be:

Boss: 'I need that project completed for my meeting on Friday morning. What day will you have it ready by?' (Step 1)

You: 'I can do it by Thursday.'

Boss: 'What time on Thursday?' (Step 2)

You: '3 p.m.' (Step 2)

Boss: 'So, on Thursday at 3 p.m. I can look on my desk and know that I'll find that report?' (Step 3)

You: '...Er, OK, yes.'

Step 3 is very important, as we are culturally quite used to saying things such as 'I'll do it by Thursday' but really meaning 'Thursday evening/Friday morning' or 'If I get in early on Friday I can finish it before the boss comes in...' Alternatively it could also mean, 'I have absolutely no intention of doing it by Thursday, but this might shut you up and get you off my back.' And we need to check if this is what the other person really means when she says, 'I'll do it by Thursday'!

Very often at the third step of the promise (ensuring that all the people involved understand what they have promised to do), the person doing the promising realizes he can't actually promise to do that, because he can't deliver on that promise. So when you ask him the checking question 'So, on Thursday at 3 p.m. I can look on my desk and know that I'll find that report?', he'll reply with, 'Well, actually, no'.

This may be a bit annoying to discover, as you really need that report. However, there are fewer things worse than the irritation and inconvenience of people making promises they have absolutely no intention of fulfilling. It's better to know that they can't do it and find an alternative solution, than to turn up empty handed to the Friday meeting.

Having established he can't get it to you by Friday, you at least know what the situation is. Now you can get to work on solving the problem.

In this case you would then use Q3, 'What would *this person* need to do to get the project completed by Friday?' or 'What would *I* need to do to ensure the project gets completed by Friday?' or, in the worst-case scenario, 'What are *we* going to need to do if this project deadline is impossible?' All of these questions move us from being stuck to finding solutions – which, by the way, is much easier to do on Monday with three days left before the meeting than on Friday with three minutes before the meeting starts.

THE DISHWASHER

As most of us have done, I took a morning off work to wait in for the delivery of my promised dishwasher. It was definitely going to be delivered between 10 a.m. and 2 p.m.

By 1 p.m. it hadn't arrived, so I rang the delivery depot to check, and was assured it was still coming. At 2.15 p.m. I rang again, and was told that the driver had had a very slow morning due to bad traffic, and would deliver it that afternoon instead. Of course it still hadn't arrived by 6 p.m. When I chased them up again I was finally told that my dishwasher wasn't on the delivery truck. And it couldn't have been, as they hadn't had any in stock for the last week; there was, in fact, no chance of me getting by dishwasher until the next week.

If only they'd told me that in the morning I could have used the day off more productively.

We've all been in similar situations. You know how this feels and how you feel about the company that's done it to you. Making good promises will make sure you don't create the opportunity for others to feel this way about you or your organization/product/service.

PROMISING YOURSELF

We can just as usefully apply this to ourselves. Q2, Q3, Q7 and Q8 will direct us to our goals and to the actions that will make those goals happen, but Q9 ensures we do the work.

Imagine your goal is to buy a second home in the Caribbean, and although you don't have the money yet, one of the actions you've decided to take is to find out what's available in that region and what it would cost. The first step would then be:

- **to phone a realtor or estate agent**

– but from what we've already learned about promises, we can tell that this is clearly not yet a promise to ourselves. However, if you define it:

- **I will phone a realtor or estate agent in the Caribbean**

– it's beginning to get closer to a promise, but it's still not quite there yet. If we further refine it to:

- I will have phoned a realtor or estate agent in the Caribbean by 6 p.m. this evening

– then now we know we have created a well-designed promise.

Now you also need to check that you've realized exactly what you have promised to do, and that you can deliver on it. Ask yourself for confirmation by saying, 'So, if someone were to ask me at 6.31 p.m. whether I had phoned a realtor or estate agent in the Caribbean, I would be able to say yes, wouldn't I?'

If the answer is a clear 'yes' then we can predict that you're going to be moving on this project this evening; if it's a 'no' then that's equally clear and you need to redesign your promise or find out what's getting in the way (and maybe use Q7 to resolve any conflict).

If it's anything else, including a suspiciously hesitant 'Er, maybe, yes?' with a large question mark after it, then you're not really sounding too committed to the promise. This can be double-checked by asking the 'Really?' question. This is a brilliant little question that asks, 'Let's be straight about this, are you really going to do that?' It produces one of two useful answers: either clarity – 'No, I am not really going to do that, am I?' – in which case we move ahead as suggested above, or an answer that reinvigorates our commitment – 'Yes, I am really going to do it!' And the promise is made!

INTEGRITY

You may also have noticed that this whole field of promises relies heavily on one very important thing: integrity. Making promises and agreements with all the right ingredients and wording doesn't mean a thing if you have no intention of keeping them.

Integrity is the quality of:

- being and keeping your word

- saying that you will do something and being able to be counted on to do it

- making it your job to find a way to do what you say you will do

- finding ways to make up for those times when you do not keep your word, when you are 'out of integrity'

- asking, 'How can I do what I have agreed to do?'

- before agreeing to do something, asking, 'Is it within my power to deliver this?'

This is an area of our lives that most of us could clean up a bit. It's possible that you have all led saintly lives and so you might be shaking your head in disagreement at that – so let's check some facts.

INTEGRITY: SAYING THAT YOU WILL DO SOMETHING AND BEING COUNTED ON TO DO IT

Exercise: Integrity Check

Have you said any of these recently?

- I'll phone you.

- I'll post it right now.

- I'll just take a minute.

- I'll be there at 6.

- We'll arrange to meet up.

- I'll get it to you by the end of the week.

– and then didn't?

Developing Integrity

Integrity issues are quite simple to fix:

- **spot them, and**

- **sort them out.**

Again, sounds simple, right? But it is, honest. Life is much less complicated when people say they're going to do something and then do it. How much of your time at work is spent chasing someone who was asked to do something and didn't? And at home, how many repetitive conversations have you had with your neighbours about parking/their pets/noise? If you have kids, how many times have you talked to them about tidying rooms/homework, etc.?

Ask yourself, 'What would it be like to live in a world of integrity, where people did what they said, first time, didn't sell me useless used cars pretending they were sound and didn't bounce cheques on me? If the rubbish collectors collected the rubbish without leaving half of it scattered outside my front door...?' Of course you'd like that.

As Gandhi suggests, 'Be the change you wish to see in the world.'

Exercise: Integrity and Promises

- Where do you need to clean up your integrity?

- What promises do you need to remake with yourself?

SUMMARY

- Make effective promises using Q9, both with yourself and others.
- Be in 'integrity'.

Phew, that's Q9, this must mean that we've reached last Question...

COMPLETION

QUESTION 10
What's Next?

'The rung of a ladder was never meant to rest upon, but only to hold a man's foot long enough to enable him to put the other somewhat higher.'
THOMAS HENRY HUXLEY

Happiness!

The Question 'What's next?' asks us to refocus all the other nine Questions onto the next stage of our project, or onto the next project itself.

It's all about planning, dealing with the unexpected, taking things step by step and having a bigger vision.

SMALL CHUNK – LARGE CHUNK

Q10 is interesting because it can be used in two very different ways:

- to focus in and examine the *smaller* bits, the details, the minutiae (small chunks) of a problem or project

- to zoom our focus out and get a sense of the larger picture (large chunks).

These two skills require different perspectives and ways of thinking; coming back to neuroplasticity, over time most people will have developed a preference for using one over the other.

Exercise: Which Are You?

Look at the points below to discover which way of thinking, small- or large-chunk, has been the one you use most, and therefore the one you tend naturally to favour, so far. When you've worked out which one you are, you can start to notice those situations in which it's an asset and also where it works against you and limits your vision. This then presents you with a great opportunity to develop new skills and behaviours.

You are likely to be a 'small-chunker' if:

- You find the idea of focusing in on the detail very intriguing, interesting, comfortable and familiar

- When asked to look at the bigger picture, the grand vision, you may feel a bit overwhelmed, confused and uncomfortable

- You like words such as 'details', 'precise', 'focused', 'specific'

- You don't use or like the large-chunkers' words much (see below).

You are likely to be a 'large-chunker' if:

- You feel freed up and excited by the idea of designing the grand plan, the big vision

- You find the idea of focusing in on the detail very uncomfortable, tiresome, restrictive and unfamiliar

- You like words such as 'open-ended', 'huge', 'free-flowing', 'big ideas'

- You don't use or like the small-chunkers' words much (see above).

Some of us will recognize ourselves as 'flexi-chunkers': we find it easy to switch from one size of focus to the other, and are happy with and use either set of words.

DEVELOPING YOUR CHUNK SIZE

It seems a truism in life that although specialism is very useful, being able to thrive in any situation and being flexible seem to be even more valuable. Being a flexi-chunker and having the ability to switch between different styles of focus seems to be an asset. This is because it allows you both to plan and appreciate the detail while also being able to design the bigger picture and keep an overview of where the whole project is going.

Exercise: Flexi-chunking

If you don't recognize yourself as a 'flexi-chunker' yet, then it's time to develop this skill.

Ask yourself Q3: 'What would I need to do to become a flexi-chunker?'

Also ask yourself the key coaching question: 'Where in my past do I recognize that I have actually used this kind of skill?'

Once again you may need to use a number of the other 10 Questions to work through this – you might have a part (Q7) of you that thinks large-chunkers are too vague about details and so let things slip; or that small-chunkers have no creative vision, stifle new ideas and so on.

Consider:

- When would it be useful for me to small-chunk more?

- When would it be useful for me to large-chunk more?

Applying Flexi-chunking

Once you've developed a familiarity with flexi-chunking, you'll be able to get even more use out of Q10.

When you are looking at the day-to-day management of a project, asking 'What do I do next?', it's usually best to do this from a small-chunk perspective that naturally encourages looking at the short term and vital details.

When looking at the development of your larger plans, asking, 'What's next in my life path?' is usually best from a larger-chunk perspective as it naturally encourages a sense of seeing the bigger picture. Answering this 'What's next in my life path?' question from a large-chunk perspective can also make the question take on a number of different time-frames. These could range from as small as a week in the future to the whole of your life (or if your personal beliefs include the idea of an existence after death, the whole of that as well).

Clearly this Question is strongly connected to Q1 'What if?' and Q8 'What am I committed to?'

Exercise: What's Next?

Ask yourself 'What's next in my life path?' and write down your answers.

What would it be like to be able to recognize your day-to-day actions as stepping-stones that form a vital part of your larger life vision?

ACHIEVING YOUR GOALS

Achieving your goals can be an opportunity to feel wonderfully fulfilled, but if you haven't used Q10 it may be a time when you feel flat and have a sense of anti-climax (most of us will have experienced this after important exams or when we leave school or a job). Having a plan of what to do next will ensure that you can enjoy the feelings of success and use them to help you build your future.

DEALING WITH THE UNEXPECTED – DANCE WITH LIFE

When the sun's shining and the birds are singing it can be quite easy to feel good, but when you've planned a picnic and you find all the shops are closed and the weather's just started like it's time for Noah to build another ark, you might not feel so light-hearted. This is one of those times when it's tempting to give in and give up, with the predictable, unhappy consequences that will have on your life.

The ability to use Q10 either before these situations occur or in the moment that everything begins to deviate from your plan is essential for being able to dance with life. Life doesn't seem to have your picnic pencilled in its diary, it hasn't arranged the weather to fit your picnicking needs, and in fact it doesn't really care either way. Life will sometimes appear to support your endeavours and other times seem out to crush them; but it's not actually bothered either way. Life doesn't have an interest, it just does what it does. If you want your life to be better than a random series of ups and downs, then you need Q10.

If the picnic is ruined by the weather, the simple Q10, 'What's next?' reminds you it's time to use Q2 and Q3, 'What do I want?', 'How am I going to get it?'

It sounds simple – and it is – but it's amazing how easy it can be to forget this when the things we've planned go up in smoke in front of our eyes. Surf over the dips in life's ups and downs with this key question, and make plans to dance with life.

I've just re-read this little section and I'm amazed at how important these few lines are; I'd say that taking on this perspective is probably one of the most important things you can ever do in life. In my interesting life so far, part of my research has meant that I've had the privilege of talking in depth with people about what makes them happy, successful, inspiring or not. Every person whom I've ever spoken with who's successful, fulfilled and happy, etc. has this perspective on life. So, if want what some of them have got, maybe you should join those who dance with what life brings!

Exercise: Dancing with Life

Take some time to imagine what it would be like to take on this habit of finding a way to dance with everything life throws at you. Whom do you know or have read about who already does this?

What would it be like to be in his or her shoes for a day?

MISUSE

'What's next?' can be misused as, 'What's going to go wrong next?' Misusing the Question in this way will have serious negative consequences for you, and in fact this is one of the key ways to get a high level of anxiety or depression running in your life. Instead, ask, 'What am I going to do next to sort this out?'

REMISSION

It has been noticed that when cancer patients recover, especially if the doctors had predicted a very poor chance of recovery, they often have a new perspective on life that motivates them to do something very different than they did before. It is usually something quite altruistic and is always something important and meaningful to them.

The medical term for this recovery from illness is 'remission', but it has been pointed out that maybe the term should be 're-mission', as the people granted this rediscover what is important to them, what their new mission in life is. It seems from my studies into what makes for happiness that having a mission is important for everyone, not just those recovering from cancer. A mission provides us with direction and meaning.

When you know what your *mission* is, then the 'What's next?' Question becomes clear. And when you ask the 'What's next in my life path?' question, your mission becomes clear.

HAPPINESS IS STRONGLY RELATED TO HAVING A MISSION IN LIFE

Exercise: What's My Mission?

Take some time now to ask yourself one of the biggest questions you can ask about yourself and your life: 'What's my mission?'

If you find yourself getting stuck, then you now have 10 great Questions to unblock yourself. I believe that everyone does have a mission; it doesn't have to be the kind of 'I will find a cure for cancer' type, although it can be. It can be a 'I want to be a fun dad for my kids,' or 'I want to get all I can out of life,' and it can of course change with time.

Then you might want to tell someone about it – but be kind to yourself and choose someone who's going to be supportive! It seems that whenever we have a goal, if we tell others about it then it instantly becomes more real and more likely to happen.

WHAT'S NEXT FOR YOU?

Remember the key point I made in the Introduction: 'When you've asked the questions and discovered the solution, then to get any benefit you must actually do something about it.' To help you with this, you need the power of the two 'A's:

1. Asking

Asking the right questions of yourself and others; having the faith in yourself and commitment to your goals to be able to ask difficult questions or to approach people and ask them for their help, feedback or insights.

2. Action

Taking on your plans and goals and putting them into action; no one else is likely to do it for you, but that's a good thing as it puts the power, the control and choices in your life back into your hands. You can take the steering wheel and you can design your future – and trust yourself, you will design it better than anyone else could.

THE FUTURE STARTS NOW

Use these powerful 10 Questions with integrity and thoughtfulness; you and the world deserve it. I look forward to hearing about what you've achieved with them and seeing and feeling the positive change in our world that results. And remember: *we are more influential in our lives than we could ever imagine.*

The table below can be used as quick reference guide to working out which of the 10 Questions you need to turn stuckness into opportunity. First work out what you've got currently using the 'got' column; then follow the columns across to see what's missing. This then should lead you to know which is the appropriate Question to ask.

got	but no	or	or	or		
stuck, a life that sucks	direction	hope	options	point	Q1	What if?
direction	clarity	motivation	goals	decision	Q2	What precisely?
clear goals	way to get them	plan of action			Q3	What can I/ would I (or you) need to do?
complaints	solutions	success			Q4	How can, not why?
negative feedback, criticism, rejection, disheartened	positives	flexibility	direction out		Q5	What am I making it mean? Reframe
conflict	resolution	energy	concentration		Q6	What does it want for me?
sabotaging behaviour	way of stopping it				Q7	What is the consequence of this? Saying NO
setbacks, dead ends	hope	focus	bigger perspective		Q8	What am I committed to?
good intentions	action	delivery			Q9	Promises/is now a good time?
completion, progress	plans, big picture	long-term goals	next step	sense of achievement	Q10	What next?

OTHER PUBLICATIONS/COURSES BY PHIL PARKER

An Introduction to the Lightning Process

This book has been designed both as an essential first step for those intending to take a Lightning Process seminar and also as a resource for discovering more about how this unique training programme can make a difference in anyone's life.

Dû – Unlock Your Full Potential with a Word

This intriguing and life-changing book explores Phil's invention of a new word that was to change the lives of thousands. This new language is a cornerstone of his Lightning Process and Peak Performance programmes. Discover in detail how and when to use these new ideas to start to get powerful change in your life.

CD AUDIO PROGRAMMES

Phil's CD titles are designed to help you with every aspect of your life, covering topics such as de-stressing, building confidence, stopping smoking, weight loss, pregnancy support and more. For a full list please visit: http://store.philparker.org

COURSES

Phil is constantly working to create new courses with easy access to all for the latest life-changing ideas. These include:

- The Dû Seminar – learning how to use the Dû

- The Lightning Process (LP)

- Phil Parker Peak Performance (P4) – for business professionals and leaders in all fields

- NLP for Business – short and longer certified courses

- Language as Medicine – a seminar for health care professionals to learn how to use words to assist the healing process

For the full and latest information please visit www.philparker.org.

▶ ▶ ▶ ▶ ▶ ▶ ▶

GLOSSARY

COACH

This is a specific type of a role that one person adopts in order to assist someone else to sort out his or her particular issues. The qualities that ensure the assistance is 'coaching' (rather than advice or interference) are:

- Coaching is only provided when there has been a request or an agreement for coaching.

- The coach leaves his own problems at the door.

- The coach clearly believes in you.

- The coach will assess the feasibility of your plans. If he believes them to be sound, he will ensure that you know that he believes that what you are aiming for is entirely possible and definitely within your ability.

- The coach always maintains a big, clear perspective, which will often be bigger and clearer than yours. This allows him to see the end-point even when you can't.

- The coach doesn't take any bull. If you've committed to achieving something and begin to cheat on yourself, talk yourself down, or not deliver on your promises, he won't stand for it.

- The coach rarely gives advice, but mainly asks questions that assist you in discovering the solutions.

- The coach is supportive and caring.

- The coach listens, but will assist you to refocus if you start to go off the point or endlessly complain.

- The coach takes the time, because he knows you're important.

- The coach has integrity; he doesn't just say things, he really means them.

- The coach ensures that you have a clear sense that he understands what is going on for you.

- The coach thinks you're important.

- The coach will give feedback instead of criticism, and will never say 'you're wrong' (this is an identity level statement, which implies *you* are wrong, rather than what you did was inappropriate), although he may suggest improvements to aspects of your performance.

- The coach is able to reflect on both his own and your performance.

- The coach brings a sense of humour and lightness to the situation.

COACHING

This describes the type of relationship where one person (the client or coachee) has very specifically and clearly asked for another person's (the coach) assistance to help her sort out a particular issue. The specific qualities that the 'coach' brings to that situation will designate it as coaching rather than advice or interference.

COMMITMENT

An outcome that you set for yourself which you dedicate yourself to in such a way that you will make happen, that you will ensure occurs, no matter what.

INFLUENCE

'Influence' is sometimes confused with 'blame' and 'responsibility', as in 'I should have influenced that,' meaning 'It's my fault' or 'I'm to blame.' But in fact, 'influence' means something quite different. It means being able to use your abilities to take action to change something, and being able to make a difference to the way things turn out. It also means that if you've promised to do something and you haven't delivered on that promise, then it's up to you to influence things (do something) to make it right.

Imagine you're on a bus and the driver collapses because he's not eaten all day. He may be at fault and to blame but he no can longer influence the situation any further; the only people left to influence it for the better, and take charge of the wheel, are all of the other passengers on the bus who can drive.

INTEGRITY

Is the quality of:

* being and keeping your word
* saying that you will do something and being able to be counted on to do it

- making sure that you find a way to do what you say you will do

- finding ways to make up for those times when you do not keep your word, when you are 'out of integrity'

- asking, 'how can I do what I have agreed to do?'

NEGATIVE OR SELF-SABOTAGING 'BEHAVIOURS'

Refers to either doing actions like sulking or saying limiting statements to ourselves such as, 'I can't,' which ensure we are less likely to get the things we really want in life.

NEURO-LINGUISTIC PROGRAMMING (NLP)

NLP is a system for finding out in detail how individuals achieve excellence, using a process called modelling. The modelling process is complete when enough detail has been discovered to teach that excellence to a novice and help her to achieve excellence in that field. NLP has modelled many skills such as spelling, speed-reading and sharp-shooting, but has also been interested in the structure that underpins depression, phobias, anxiety, allergies, etc. Learning about how we 'do' these things well allows us to teach people who currently excel at these 'skills' (depression, phobias, stress or allergies) to become less proficient, to the point where they don't have the problem anymore.

OUTCOMES

These are similar to goals that we set ourselves in life, but outcomes are distinguished by having a much greater degree of thoughtfulness and specificity that makes them much more likely to be attained. Q2 will ensure you create outstanding outcomes.

PROMISES AND AGREEMENTS

Contracts that are clear to all parties involved and have specific, measurable results that can be verified at a certain date.

STRATEGY

A series of thoughts, actions and behaviours that we consistently use to deal with particular kinds of situations. We design strategies to cope with new situations or at times when we don't know quite what to do or how to behave. At the time these strategies are the best response to that situation that we can dream up. Later on in life they may be much less appropriate than they were when we first designed them, for example the strategy of having a temper tantrum when you don't get what you want or things don't turn out as you hoped may be useful for a child, but will be a liability for a salesperson or surgeon!

EXERCISE ANSWERS

QUESTION 2

Exercise: Stating It in Positives

- 'Not fear and dread' – becomes, for example, 'Calm and confident'

- 'Not to be made redundant' – becomes, for example, 'Keep this job or find an even better, brilliant one'

- 'Not sad' – becomes, for example, 'Happy'

- 'Not helpless' – becomes, for example, 'Empowered'

- 'Not to feel bad about myself and beat myself up' – becomes, for example, 'Kind to myself, see the positives in what I do'

- 'Not expecting everything to be difficult' – becomes, for example, 'Expecting things to work out brilliantly'

Exercise: Q2

'I get bored and put off any project I take on.'

Q: So what precisely do you want, in positives?

A: I want to find a project I am really enthusiastic about, stay focused, interested and committed to it and create a strategy to make sure I am motivated, so I start and complete it in the time scale I set myself.

QUESTION 5

Exercise: Look for Red

- Having written down the things you remember in the room that were red, now write down what you saw that was green, blue and brown.

You will probably have found this quite difficult. Even though you scanned the room closely for 5 seconds, research shows that you will not have remembered seeing much in the room that wasn't red because, even though your *eyes* saw everything, your *mind* was busy looking for red things and filtered out what it considered irrelevant. This is the way our brain deals with the immense amount of information presented to it every second of our lives:

- If we are looking for something, we will see it, even if it's not there. Do you ever remember breaking up with a partner and then thinking you see them everywhere, but you're just superimposing them on other people who vaguely share a common feature with that lost partner?
- We often don't see things that we're not looking for.
- If we keep on finding the same things turning up in our lives, there's a good chance it's because we've

been looking for them; so look at what happens in your life; work out what you must have been looking for to find that, and decide whether that is the focus you want to have for your future. If not, maybe it's time to change your focus.

REFERENCES

QUESTION 1

1. R Dilts, *Strategies of Genius* (vol 1; Meta Publications, 1994)

QUESTION 2

1. B S Siegel, *Love, Medicine and Miracles: Lessons Learned About Self-Healing from a Surgeon's Experience with Exceptional Patients* (New York: Harper Perennial, 1986), page 133. It is not stated that the trial participants had cancer, just that they were testing the drug.
2. L Watson, *Supernature* (Coronet Books, 1974), page 87

QUESTION 7

1. S Covey, *The 7 Habits of Highly Effective People* (Simon & Schuster, 2004)

PRAISE FOR
THE TEN QUESTIONS TO ASK FOR SUCCESS

'In this concise and engaging manual Phil Parker manages to deliver the key elements for creating change and managing the challenges of business and personal life. The genius idea of this book is that it transforms these change concepts into simple, understandable, practical, universal questions. I highly recommend this book to everyone interested in personal and professional development and success.'

STEVE ANDREAS, NLP AUTHOR AND DEVELOPER

'Phil Parker has an amazing toolbox of skills to help you get the best out of yourself, whatever your challenge.'

ED STAFFORD, FIRST MAN EVER TO WALK THE ENTIRE LENGTH OF THE AMAZON

JOIN THE HAY HOUSE FAMILY

As the leading self-help, mind, body and spirit publisher in the UK, we'd like to welcome you to our family so that you can enjoy all the benefits our website has to offer.

 EXTRACTS from a selection of your favourite author titles

 COMPETITIONS, PRIZES & SPECIAL OFFERS Win extracts, money off, downloads and so much more

 LISTEN to a range of radio interviews and our latest audio publications

 CELEBRATE YOUR BIRTHDAY An inspiring gift will be sent your way

 **LATEST NEWS** Keep up with the latest news from and about our authors

 **ATTEND OUR AUTHOR EVENTS** Be the first to hear about our author events

 iPHONE APPS Download your favourite app for your iPhone

 HAY HOUSE INFORMATION Ask us anything, all enquiries answered

join us online at **www.hayhouse.co.uk**

  292B Kensal Road, London W10 5BE
T: 020 8962 1230 E: info@hayhouse.co.uk

ABOUT THE AUTHOR

Phil Parker DO Dip E Hyp P NLP MBIH Certified Master Practitioner of NLP is an internationally renowned lecturer, therapist and innovator in the field of personal development. He has also changed the lives of thousands of people by designing the groundbreaking Lightning Process® seminars.

His core principle is that people are geniuses with amazing skills, qualities and talents, and he hopes he can help as many people as possible to find that out about themselves. You can get Phil's latest thoughts, self-help tools and videos for free from his podcast, blog, Twitter and Facebook sites.

This book was the starting point of the journey that led him to design The Lightning Process, a powerful process for change which has already transformed and enhanced the lives, health and success of thousands of people around the world.

phil@philparker.org